# Canadian Corrections Officer Study Guide

## CSC Correctional Officer Study Guide with Practice Questions

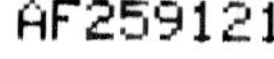

**Please note that the Corrections Officer test is administered by Correctional Service of Canada, which was not involved in the production of, and does not endorse, this product.**

**All material presented here is for SKILL PRACTICE ONLY.**

ISBN-13: 9781772453294

Version 8 March 2021

# About Complete Test Preparation Inc.

The Complete Test Preparation Team has been publishing high quality study materials since 2005. Over one million students visit our websites every year, and thousands of students, teachers and parents all over the world (over 100 countries) have purchased our teaching materials, curriculum, study guides and practice tests.

Complete Test Preparation Inc. is committed to providing students with the best study materials and practice tests available on the market. Members of our team combine years of teaching experience, with experienced writers and editors, all with advanced degrees.

https://www.test-preparation.ca

https://www.facebook.com/CompleteTestPreparation/

https://www.youtube.com/user/MrTestPreparation

# CONTENTS

# Getting Started

CONGRATULATIONS! By deciding to take the CSC Corrections Officer Test, you have taken the first step toward a great future! Of course, there is no point in taking this important examination unless you intend to do your best to earn the highest grade you possibly can. That means getting yourself organized and discovering the best approaches, methods and strategies to master the material. Yes, that will require real effort and dedication on your part, but if you are willing to focus your energy and devote the study time necessary, before you know it you will be on you way to a brighter future.

We know that taking on a new endeavour can be scary, and it is easy to feel unsure of where to begin. That's where we come in. This study guide is designed to help you improve your test-taking skills, show you a few tricks of the trade and increase both your competency and confidence.

## The CSC Corrections Officer Test

The Corrections Officer Test  has  three modules, English Language Arts and Math.  The English Language Arts consists of English grammar and usage, vocabulary and an essay.  The Math module contains basic High School math.

While we seek to make our guide as comprehensive as possible, note that like all entrance exams, the Corrections Officer Test might be adjusted at some future point. New material might be added, or content that is no longer relevant or applicable might be removed. It is always a good idea to give the materials you receive when you register to take the Test a careful review.

# HOW THIS STUDY GUIDE IS ORGANIZED

This study guide is divided into three sections. The first section, Self-Assessments, which will help you recognize your areas of strength and weaknesses. This will be a boon when it comes to managing your study time most efficiently; there is not much point of focusing on material you have already got firmly under control. Instead, taking the self-assessments will show you where that time could be much better spent. In this area you will begin with a few questions to evaluate quickly your understanding of material that is likely to appear on the Corrections Officer Test. If you do poorly in certain areas, simply work carefully through those sections in the tutorials and then try the self-assessment again.

The second section, Tutorials, offers information in each of the content areas, as well as strategies to help you master that material. The tutorials are not intended to be a complete course, but cover general principles. If you find that you do not understand the tutorials, it is recommended that you seek out additional instruction.

Third, we offer two sets of practice test questions, similar to those on the test. Again, we cover all modules, so make sure to check with your school!

# THE CORRECTIONS OFFICER TEST STUDY PLAN

Now that you have made the decision to take the test, it is time to get started. Before you do another thing, you will need to figure out a plan of attack. The best study tip is to start early! The longer the time period you devote to regular study practice, the likelier that you will retain the material and access it quickly. If you thought that 1 x 20 is the same as 2 x 10, guess what? It really is not, when it comes to study time. Reviewing material for just an hour per day over the course of 20 days is far better than studying for two hours a day for only 10 days. The more often you revisit a particular piece of information, the better you will know it. Not only will your grasp and understanding be better, but your ability to reach into your brain and quickly and efficiently pull out the tidbit you need, will be greatly enhanced as well.

The great Chinese scholar and philosopher Confucius believed that true knowledge could be defined as knowing what you know and what you do not know. The first step in preparing for the test is to assess your strengths and weaknesses. You may already have an idea of what you know and what you do not know, but evaluating yourself using our Self- Assessment modules for each of the three areas, Math, English and Reading Comprehension, will clarify the details.

## Making a Study Schedule

To make your study time the most productive, you will need to develop a study plan. The purpose of the plan is to organize all the bits of pieces of information in such a way that you will not feel overwhelmed. Rome was not built in a day, and learning everything you will need to know to pass the Corrections Officer Test is going to take time, too. Arranging the material you need to learn into manageable chunks is the best way to go. Each study session should make you feel as though you have accomplished your goal, or at least are a little closer, and your goal is simply to learn what you planned to learn during that particular session. Try to organize the content in such a way that each study session builds on previous ones. That way, you will retain the information, be better able to access it, and review the previous bits and pieces at the same time.

## Self-assessment

**The Best Study Tip!** The best study tip is to start early! The longer you study regularly, the more you will retain and 'learn' the material. Studying for 1 hour per day for 20 days is far better than studying for 2 hours for 10 days.

**What don't you know?**

The first step is to assess your strengths and weaknesses. You may already have an idea of where your weaknesses are, or you can take our Self-assessment modules for each of the areas, WCPT and Situational Judgement.

| Exam Component | Rate from 1 to 5 |
|---|---|
| | |
| **English / Language Arts** | |
| Vocabulary | |
| Grammar & Usage | |
| Punctuation | |
| Capitalization | |
| Main Idea | |
| Reading | |
| Summarizing | |
| | |
| **Situational  Judgement** | |
| | |

## Making a Study Schedule

The key to a successful study plan is to divide the material you need to learn into manageable size and learn it, while at the same time reviewing the material that you already know.

Using the table above, any scores of three or below, mean you need to spend time learning, reviewing and practicing this subject area.  A score of four means you need to review the material, but you don't have to spend time re-learning. A score of five and you are OK with just an occasional review before the exam.

A score of zero or one means you really do need to work on this and you should allocate the most time and give it the highest priority. Some students prefer a 5-day plan and others a 10-day plan. It also depends on how much time you have until the exam.

Here is an example of a 5-day plan based on an example from the table above:

**Punctuation:** 1   Study 1 hour everyday – review on last day
**Main Idea:** 3   Study 1 hour for 2 days then ½ hour and then review
**Vocabulary:**  4   Review every second day
**Grammar & Usage:** 2 Study 1 hour on the first day – then ½ hour everyday
**Reading Comprehension:**  5   Review for ½ hour every other day
**Situational Judgement:**  5 Review for ½ hour every other day

Using this example, Situational Judgement and reading comprehension are good and only need occasional review. Vocabulary is good and needs 'some' review. Main Idea need a bit of work, grammar and usage needs a lot of work and Punctuation is very weak and need most time.  Based on this, here is a sample study plan:

| Day | Subject | Time |
|---|---|---|
|  |  |  |
| **Monday** |  |  |
| Study | Punctuation | 1 hour |
| Study | Grammar & Usage | 1 hour |
| **½ hour break** |  |  |
| Study | Main Idea | 1 hour |
| Review | Vocabulary | ½ hour |
|  |  |  |
| **Tuesday** |  |  |
| Study | Punctuation | 1 hour |
| Study | Grammar & Usage | ½ hour |

|  | ½ hour break |  |
|---|---|---|
| Study | Main Idea | ½ hour |
| Review | Vocabulary | ½ hour |
| Review | Situational Judgement | ½ hour |
|  |  |  |
| **Wednesday** |  |  |
| Study | Punctuation | 1 hour |
| Study | Grammar & Usage | ½ hour |
|  | ½ hour break |  |
| Study | Main Idea | ½ hour |
| Review | Situational Judgement | ½ hour |
|  |  |  |
| **Thursday** |  |  |
| Study | Punctuation | ½ hour |
| Study | Grammar & Usage | ½ hour |
| Review | Main Idea | ½ hour |
|  | ½ hour break |  |
| Review | Situational Judgement | ½ hour |
| Review | Vocabulary | ½ hour |
|  |  |  |
| **Friday** |  |  |
| Review | Punctuation | ½ hour |
| Review | Grammar & Usage | ½ hour |
| Review | Main Idea | ½ hour |
|  | ½ hour break |  |
| Review | Vocabulary | ½ hour |
| Review | Grammar & Usage | ½ hour |

Using this example, adapt the study plan to your own schedule. This schedule assumes 2 ½ - 3 hours available to study everyday for a 5 day period.

First, write out what you need to study and how much. Next figure out how many days you have before the test. Note, do NOT study on the last day before the test. On the last day before the test, you won't learn anything and will probably only confuse yourself.

Make a table with the days before the test and the number of hours you have available to study each day. We suggest working with 1 hour and ½ hour time slots.

Start filling in the blanks, with the subjects you need to study the most getting the most time and the most regular time slots (i.e. everyday) and the subjects that you know getting the least time (e.g. ½ hour every other day, or every 3rd day).

# Tips for making a schedule

**Once you make a schedule, stick with it!**  Make your study sessions reasonable.   If you make a study schedule and don't stick with it, you set yourself up for failure.  Instead, schedule study sessions that are a bit shorter and set yourself up for success!  Make sure your study sessions are do-able.  Studying is hard work but after you pass, you can party and take a break!

**Schedule breaks.**  Breaks are just as important as study time.  Work out a rotation of studying and breaks that works for you.

**Build up study time.**   If you find it hard to sit still and study for 1 hour straight through, build up to it.  Start with 20 minutes, and then take a break.  Once you get used to 20-minute study sessions, increase the time to 30 minutes.  Gradually work you way up to 1 hour.

**40 minutes to 1 hour is optimal**.   Studying for longer than this is tiring and not productive.  Studying for shorter isn't long enough to be productive.

**Studying Math.**   Studying Math is different from studying other subjects because you use a different part of your brain.  The best way to study math is to practice everyday.  This will train your mind to think in a mathematical way.  If you miss a day or days, the mathematical mind-set is gone and you have to start all over again to build it up.

Study and practice math everyday for at least 5 days before the exam.

# WCPT



THIS SECTION CONTAINS A SELF-ASSESSMENT AND TUTORIALS. The tutorials are designed to familiarize general principles and the self-assessment contains general questions similar to the questions likely to be on the Corrections Officer Test, but are not intended to be identical to the exam questions. The tutorials are not designed to be a complete course, and it is assumed that students have some familiarity with these questions. If you do not understand parts of the tutorial, or find the tutorial difficult, it is recommended that you seek out additional instruction.

Note that these questions are for skill practice only.

## TOUR OF THE WCPT CONTENT

Below is a detailed list of the types of questions that generally appear on the test.

- Identifying grammar mistakes

- Choosing the best title for a passage

- Sentence and paragraph order

- Summarizing

- Punctuation

- Vocabulary

- English usage

- Avoiding wordiness and redundancy

- Main idea and details

The questions below are not the same as you will find on the WCPT - that would be too easy! And nobody knows what the questions will be and they change all the time.  Mostly the changes consist of substituting new questions for old, but the changes can be new question formats or styles, changes to the number of questions in each section, changes to the time limits for each section and combining sections.  Below are general reading questions that cover the same areas as the WCPT.  So, while the format and exact wording of the questions may differ slightly, and change from year to year, if you can answer the questions below, you will have no problem with the reading section of the WCPT.

# WCPT SELF-ASSESSMENT

The purpose of the self-assessment is:

- Identify your strengths and weaknesses.

- Develop your personalized study plan (above)

- Get accustomed to the WCPT format

- Extra practice – the self-assessments are almost a full $3^{rd}$ practice test!

- Provide a baseline score for preparing your study schedule.

Since this is a Self-assessment, and depending on how

confident you are with Reading Comprehension, timing is optional. The WCPT has 35 reading questions. The self-assessment has 12 questions, so allow about 15 minutes to complete this assessment.

Once complete, use the table below to assess your understanding of the content, and prepare your study schedule described in chapter 1.

| | |
|---|---|
| 80% - 100% | Excellent – you have mastered the content |
| 60 – 79% | Good. You have a working knowledge. Even though you can just pass this section, you may want to review the Tutorials and do some extra practice to see if you can improve your mark. |
| 40% - 59% | Below Average. You do not understand the reading comprehension problems.<br><br>Review the tutorials, and retake this quiz again in a few days, before proceeding to the rest of the Practice Test Questions. |
| Less than 40% | Poor. You have a very limited understanding of the reading comprehension problems.<br><br>Please review the Tutorials, and retake this quiz again in a few days, before proceeding to the Practice Test Questions. |

# ORDERING SENTENCES

1. __ __ __ __ __

2. __ __ __ __ __

3. __ __ __ __ __

4. __ __ __ __ __

5. __ __ __ __ __

# READING, AND SENTENCE CORRECTION

|    | A | B | C | D |
|----|---|---|---|---|
| 1  | ○ | ○ | ○ | ○ |
| 2  | ○ | ○ | ○ | ○ |
| 3  | ○ | ○ | ○ | ○ |
| 4  | ○ | ○ | ○ | ○ |
| 5  | ○ | ○ | ○ | ○ |
| 6  | ○ | ○ | ○ | ○ |
| 7  | ○ | ○ | ○ | ○ |
| 8  | ○ | ○ | ○ | ○ |
| 9  | ○ | ○ | ○ | ○ |
| 10 | ○ | ○ | ○ | ○ |

**Instructions Questions 1 - 5:** The first sentence of a paragraph is given below, followed by additional sentences in the paragraph, listed in no particular order. Order the sentences to create the best paragraph. Make sure the paragraph is properly organized and grammatically correct.

**1. Scientists that have been studying sleep have determined that teens need more sleep than they currently get.**

A. At school, teens have difficulty with complex thought because many of them do not get enough sleep each night.

B. Research determined that sleep is necessary to help with creating memories and solving problems.

C. To help teens get more sleep, many schools are pushing back their start times so their students perform better.

D. Along with difficulty thinking, teens who do not get enough sleep can have more stress in their lives, simply due to an increase in cortisol, the hormone that causes stress.

E. In response to the high levels of stress in the body, teens also act impulsively and they can lose their sense of humor.

**2. Concussion laws are changing the way that many sports are played, but many people do not know very much about concussions at all.**

A. While the intensity of the impact may or may not cause a concussion, researchers have found that when athletes are hit on the top of the head they are more likely to suffer from a concussion.

B. Many people believe that concussions only occur when athletes are hit on the head.

C. In reality, concussions can occur if direct impact occurs on the face or neck as well as anywhere else that the force can be sent to the head.

D. Due to the uncertainty of whether or not an  impact has actually caused a concussion is the major reason why concussion laws have been enacted.

E. One of the scariest things about concussions is that they happen with varying degrees of impact.

**3. Homecoming celebrations have been held at colleges and high schools across the United States since the mid-1800s.**

A. Even though other schools think they had homecoming games prior to Missouri, the reason that Missouri has the title is because the athletic director invited alumni to come home to see a big game between Kansas and Missouri in 1911.

B. Despite the NCAA giving Missouri the official designation of having the first homecoming, Baylor University claims one of the earliest homecomings with activities for alumni that included an afternoon football game along with reunion parties and a parade.

C. The actual origins of the traditional event are unknown, but the University of Missouri is the homecoming birthplace as stated by the NCAA.

D. The first true homecoming may never be known, but what is known for sure is that most colleges and high schools did not hold homecoming celebrations in 1918 due to World War I.

E. The University of Illinois also claims to have had an earlier homecoming celebration than the one in Missouri.

**4. William Howard Taft was an unlikely president who served from 1909 until 1913.**

A. The biggest weakness  was that he was morbidly obese weighing in at 335 pounds on his 6 foot 2 frame.

B. His obesity caused him to suffer from health problems like sleep apnea.

C.  Despite his strengths, he had many weaknesses.

D. It also caused him to get stuck in the White House bathtub, which prompted him to have a tub installed that could fit four fully grown men.

E.  As president, he was knowledgeable about the law and fighting for the good of the country.

**5. The Apollo Space Program was one of the most important scientific programs in the history of the United States.**

A. The first Apollo missions was manned, but never left the ground due to a fire that ended the life of Gus Grissom, Edward White, and Roger Chaffee.

B. The highlight of the program was Apollo 11, which was the flight where Neil Armstrong, Michael Collins, and Buzz Aldrin landed on the moon in the Sea of Tranquility.

C. After several test launches, the seventh mission, called Apollo 7, resulted in the first manned orbit of the Earth.

D. Even though the mission did not go as planned, Apollo 13 showed the world what NASA was made of as scientists worked together to bring three astronauts on a heavily damaged orbiter safely back to Earth.

E. Following the Apollo 1 disaster, NASA scientists had to reevaluate the safety of the program.

# READING

**Question 1 refers to the following passage.**

**Was Dr. Seuss a Real Doctor?**

A favorite author for over 100 years, Theodor Seuss Geisel
was born on March 2, 1902. Today, we celebrate the birthday of the famous "Dr. Seuss" by hosting Read Across America events throughout the March. School children around
the country celebrate the "Doctor's" birthday by making
hats, giving presentations and holding read aloud circles
featuring some of Dr. Seuss' most famous books.

But who was Dr. Seuss? Did he go to medical school? Where
was his office? You may be surprised to know that Theodor
Seuss Geisel was not a medical doctor at all. He took on
the nickname Dr. Seuss when he became a noted children's
book author. He earned the nickname because people said
his books were "as good as medicine." All these years later,
his nickname has lasted and he is known as Dr. Seuss all
across the world.

Think back to when you were a young child. Did you ever
want to try "green eggs and ham?" Did you try to "Hop on
Pop?" Do you remember learning about the environment
from a creature called The Lorax? Of course, you must recall
one of Seuss' most famous characters; that green Grinch
who stole Christmas. These stories were all written by Dr.
Seuss and featured his signature rhyming words and letters.
They also featured made up words to enhance his rhyme
scheme and even though many of his characters were made
up, they sure seem real to us today.

And what of his "signature" book, The Cat in the Hat? You
must remember that cat and Thing One and Thing Two from
your childhood. Did you know that in the early 1950's there
was a growing concern in America that children were not
becoming avid readers? This was, book publishers thought,
because children found books dull and uninteresting. An

intelligent publisher sent Dr. Seuss a book of words that he thought all children should learn as young readers. Dr. Seuss wrote his famous story The Cat in the Hat, using those words.  We can see, over the decades, just how much influence his writing has had on very young children. That is why we celebrate this doctor's birthday each March.

**1. The theme of this passage is**

    a. Dr. Seuss was not a doctor.

    b. Dr. Seuss influenced the lives of generations of young children.

    c. Dr. Seuss wrote rhyming books.

    d. Dr. Seuss' birthday is a good day to read a book.

**Question 2 refers to the following passage.**

**The Civil War**

The Civil War began on April 12, 1861. The first shots of the Civil War were fired in Fort Sumter, South Carolina.  Note that even though more American lives were lost in the Civil War than in any other war, not one person died on that first day.  The war began because eleven Southern states seceded from the Union and tried to start their own government, The Confederate States of America.

Why did the states secede? The issue of slavery was a primary cause of the Civil War. The eleven southern states relied heavily on their slaves to foster their farming and plantation lifestyles. The northern states, many of whom had already abolished slavery, did not feel that the southern states should have slaves. The north wanted to free all the slaves and President Lincoln's goal was to both end slavery and preserve the Union. He had Congress declare war on the Confederacy on April 14, 1862. For four long, blood soaked years, the North and South fought.

From 1861 to mid 1863, it seemed as if the South would win this war. However, on July 1, 1863, an epic three day battle was waged on a field in Gettysburg, Pennsylvania. Gettysburg is remembered for being the bloodiest battle in American history. At the end of the three days, the North turned the tide of the war in their favour.

The North then went on to dominate the South for the remainder of the war. A famous episode is General Sherman's "March to The Sea," where he famously led the Union Army through Georgia and the Carolinas, burning and destroying everything in their path.

In 1865, the Union army invaded and captured the Confederate capital of Richmond Virginia. Robert E. Lee, leader of the Confederacy surrendered to General Ulysses S. Grant, leader of the Union forces, on April 9, 1865. The Civil War was over and the Union was preserved.

**2. Which of the following statements summarizes a FACT from the passage?**

> a. Congress declared war and then the Battle of Fort Sumter began.
>
> b. Congress declared war after shots were fired at Fort Sumter.
>
> c. President Lincoln was pro slavery
>
> d. President Lincoln was at Fort Sumter with Congress

**Questions 3 refers to the following passage.**

**Hansel and Gretel**

. . . The boy was called Hansel and the girl Gretel. He had little to bite and to break, and once when great dearth fell on the land, he could no longer procure even daily bread. Now when he thought over this by night in his bed, and tossed about in his anxiety, he groaned and said to his wife: 'What is to become of us? How are we to feed our poor children, when we no longer have anything even for ourselves?' 'I'll tell you what, husband,' answered the woman, 'early tomorrow morning we will take the children out into the forest to where it is the thickest; there we will light a fire for them, and give each of them one more piece of bread, and then we will go to our work and leave them alone. They will not find the way home again, and we shall be rid of them.' 'No, wife,' said the man, 'I will not do that; how can I bear to leave my children alone in the forest?—the wild animals would soon come and tear them to pieces.' 'O, you fool!' said she, 'then we must all four die of hunger, you may as well plane the planks for our coffins,' and she left him no peace until he consented . . . .

from *Hansel and Gretel by Jacob and Wilhelm Grimm*

## 3. Which of the following is the best topic sentence for the passage?

a.  There once was a rich man who dwelt in a great forest with his wife and his two children.

b.  Close to a great forest dwelt a poor wood-cutter with his wife and his two children.

c.  Once upon a time, deep in the forest, dwelt a happy, loving family with two children.

d.  The Black Forest was home to a king and his two children, a boy and a girl.

## Question 4 refers to the following passage.

### Boys on an Island

. . . Then they cooked some bacon in the frying pan and used up half of their corn bread. It was glorious to feast on an unexplored, uninhabited island. The boys agreed that they never would return to civilization. The fire lit their faces and threw its reddish glare on tree trunks and vines . . . .

from *The Adventures of Tom Sawyer by Mark Twain*

## 4. Which of the following is the best first sentence for the passage?

a. Tom had procured some bacon from his aunt to be used as sustenance for the day's adventure.

b. Tom and Huck avoided school that morning and went into town for supplies.

c. They built a fire alongside a large log about twenty steps inside the forest.

d. They had always enjoyed paddling down river looking for campsites.

# SENTENCE CORRECTION

## A Personal Satellite?

### Questions 5 - 8 refer to the following passage

Many of us are already so loaded with technology, we don't have  time to think about integrating even more! [1] In fact at this point it seems impossible to think about personal satellites now, just as we once thought about smart phones. [2] The reality of personal spacecraft is still in the realm of Star Trek and geeky space fantasies. [3]

However, the days when each of us will have our own personal satellite are not far away! [4] And what is even more exciting is they will be available for the cost of an iPhone! [5] At least, according to Zach Manchester, the inventor of the nano-satellite KickSat. [6] "I'd like to think of it as the people's satellite," says Manchester. [7] "We're pushing towards a personal satellite, where you can afford to put your own thing in space." [8]

The KickSat, a 30 cm. long hardware pack, is a space enthusiast's dream. [9] It contains the basics of a fully functional satellite. [10] Inside its compact design, the KickSat itself contains 200 more tinier satellites of cubic shape called "Sprites." [11] The Sprites are engineered and programmed so that they can be tracked and communicate via radio signals with a ground station on earth. [12] Each Sprite is available for purchase and is uniquely named after the sponsors who support Zach's project. [13] Anyone who has sponsored a Sprite will be able to track their personal satellite from a ground station installed in their balcony or roof! [14]

**5. Which sentence from the passage is an example of a sentence fragment?**

    a. 4

    b. 7

    c. 6

    d. 10

**6. Which of the following sentences should be edited to reduce redundancy?**

    a. 5

    b. 4

    c. 10

    d. 16

**7. Which of the following changes are needed to sentence 2?**

    a. In fact at this point it seems impossible to think about personal satellites now - just as we once thought about smart phones.

    b. In fact, at this point, it seems impossible to think about personal satellites now, just as we once thought about smart phones.

    c. In fact, at this point, it seems impossible to think about personal satellites now - just as we once thought about smart phones.

    d. In fact at this point, it seems impossible to think about personal satellites now, just as we once thought about smart phones.

**8. Which of the following changes are needed to sentence 11?**

a. Under its compact design, the KickSat itself contains 200 more tiny satellites of cubic shape called "Sprites."

b. Under its compact design, the KickSat itself contains 200 more tiny satellites of cubic shapes called "Sprites."

c. Inside its compact design, the KickSat itself contains 200 tinier satellites of cubic shapes called "Sprites."

d. With its compact design, the KickSat contains 200 tiny cube-shaped satellites called "Sprites."

## Alvin Lee's Guitar

**Questions 9 and 10 refer to the following passage**

Only a few of his contemporaries rocked the rock n' roll era with their guitars like Alvin Lee. [1] Even at the age of 67, just a year before his demise, he produced one of the finest albums of his five-decade long career with *Still on the Road to Freedom.* [2] Strikingly flamboyant with his guitar, Lee gained millions of admirers around the world with hits like "*I'd Love to Change the World*," "*On the Road to Freedom*" and "*Freedom for the Stallion*" which reflected popular worldviews at the time of their release. [3]

Alvin Lee began playing guitar at an early age, and was influenced by his parents' passion for music and inspired by the likes of Chuck Berry and Scotty Moore. [4] Lee started his career as the lead vocalist and guitarist in a band named the Jaybirds at the famous Marquee Club in London in 1962. [5] A few years later the band changed its name to *Ten Years After* and released its debut album under the new name. [6] Lee's lightning fast guitar playing at the Woodstock Festival gained him instant stardom and Lee was asked to tour the US. [7]

In the coming years, he worked with rock legends like Mylon LeFevre, George Harrison, Steve Winwood, Ronnie Wood and

Mick Fleetwood and released the country rock masterpiece *On the Road to Freedom* which brought him overwhelming trans-Atlantic popularity. [8] In subsequent years, he continued addressing social and global issues in albums like *A Space in Time, Pump Iron!, Let It Rock* and *Rocket Fuel.* [9] With many of his songs, such as, "*I'd Love to Change the World,*" Lee used the power of rock music to show his solidarity with ordinary people and their worldviews. [10] He also went on with inspiring the upcoming generations of rock stars by producing expressive and tasteful guitar performances in his 1980s albums *Free Fall, RX5* and *Detroit Diesel.* [11]

**9. Which sentence in the second paragraph is the least relevant to the main idea of the second paragraph?**

    a. 4

    b. 5

    c. 6

    d. 7

**10. Which of the following sentences, if inserted before sentence 11, would best illustrate the main idea of the passage?**

a. His charismatic personality earned him more fame and led him to perform even better for the sake of his admirers.

b. As he gained popularity because of his artistic creations he tried to implant political motives into his music.

c. At the same time, he thought of doing something for the future generations.

d. With the creative songs he composed, he established himself as an exemplary figure among fellow guitarists and the generations that followed.

# ANSWER KEY

# SENTENCE ORDER

## 1. B A D E C

Sentence B follows the topic sentence by sharing the problems that can come from a lack of sleep. Sentence A provides more information teens and their troubles with problem solving. D uses a transition that should follow the sentence about problem solving. Sentence E also uses a transitional phrase that provides more information about stress levels that are shared in sentence D. Sentence C provides closure and a solution to the problem.

## 2. B C E A D

Sentence B ties back to the first sentence by explaining what people know about concussions. Sentence C clears up the inaccuracies that people have about concussions. Sentence E explains the first reason why concussions are so frightening. Sentence A has a transition that refers back to sentence E. Sentence D provides a conclusion to the paragraph by referring back to why the laws were created.

## 3. C B E A D

Sentence C provides a fact that appropriately follows the topic sentence. Sentence B uses a transition that needs to follow sentence C. Sentence E includes the words "also claims" which means it should follow the information in sentence B. Sentence A explains why B and E are not given the title of first homecoming school. Sentence D shares information about all the schools that had early homecomings.

## 4. E C A B D

Sentence E fits after the topic sentence because it talks about what he was good at as president. Sentence C has a transition that must follow sentence E. Sentence A shares his biggest weakness, which fits after C. Sentence B refers back to his obesity. Sentence D contains the word "also" and provides another detail about his obesity.

## 5. A E C B D

Sentence A is the first sentence because it addresses the first Apollo mission. Sentence E uses the transition "following" to show that it is chronologically after the 1st sentence. Sentence C chronologically fits because it is the closest number to one. Sentence B includes Apollo 11, which is in chronological order. Sentence  D is about Apollo 13, which is the largest number and should be last in the sentence.

# READING AND USAGE

## 1. B
The passage describes in detail how Dr. Seuss had a great effect on the lives of children through his writing. It names several of his books, tells how he helped children become avid readers and explains his style of writing.

Choice A is incorrect  because that is just one single fact about the passage. Choice C is incorrect  because that is just one single fact about the passage.  Choice D is incorrect because that is just one single fact about the passage. Again, choice B is correct because it encompasses ALL the facts in the passage, not just one single fact.

## 2. B
Look at the dates in the passage. The shots were fired on April 12 and Congress declared war on April 14.

Choice C is incorrect because the passage states that Lincoln was against slavery.  Choice D is incorrect because it never mentions who was or was not at Fort Sumter.

## 3. B
Choice B matches the rest of the paragraph: a poor family with two children.

Choice A is incorrect because the family is clearly not rich; they are starving.

Choice C is incorrect because, although the family and children are right, the parents are neither happy nor loving.

Choice D is incorrect because the rest of the paragraph shows that they are not royalty. This choice is plausible because of the flow of "a boy and a girl" into the next sentence, but incorrect.

### 4. C
This flows into the paragraph.

Choice A does not flow into the rest of the paragraph, but is plausible because it mentions the same food. Choice B is incorrect because the rest of the paragraph takes place on an uninhabited island, not in town. Choice D is incorrect because it jumps from talking about their mind-set on the river right into cooking food on the island.

## CORRECTION SENTENCES

### 5. C
Sentence 6 is a fragment. "At least, according to Zach Manchester, the inventor of the nano-satellite KickSat."

This sentence fails to complete the thought, even though it is somewhat consistent with the previous sentence. Sentence 6 does not have a subject and thus does not form any main clause which is essential for constructing a complete thought. This fragment can be revised as "At least, this is according to Zach Manchester, the inventor of the nano-satellite KickSat."

### 6. B
Suggested changes to Sentence 4 to reduce redundancy, "However, the days when each of us will have our own personal spacecraft are truly not far away!"

The adjectives "own" and "personal" are used simultaneously. Either of them can be used, and the other must be eliminated. The correct form will be either one of the following:

- However, the days when each of us will have our own spacecraft are truly not far away!
- However, the days when each of us will have our personal spacecraft are truly not far away!

## 7. C

The revised version of sentence 2 is, "In fact, at this point, it seems impossible to think about personal satellites now - just as we once thought about smart phones."

This choice uses the correct punctuation; two commas, one before and one after the subordinate conjunction "at this point" which bridges the adverbial clause after it with the adjective at the start of the sentence. Also the use of a hyphen to express extended thought is correct in choice C.

## 8. D

The only choice with correct grammar is choice D. It replaces "more tiny" with "tiny" as well as "cubic shaped" with "cube-shaped." Tinier is the correct comparative form of "tiny" and "cubic" is the adjective that must describe the singular noun "shape," not "shapes" or any of its verbal forms. Two word adjectives, such as "a 3-mile race" are hyphenated.

"Under its compact design" is incorrect.  Replace with, "with its compact design ... "

## 9. A

Sentence 4 is least relevant, "Alvin Lee began playing guitar at an early age, and was influenced by his parents' passion for music and inspired by the likes of Chuck Berry and Scotty Moore."

This sentence talks about Lee's source of motivation rather than his achievements, which is actually the main topic of the paragraph. Other sentences are related to a significant extent, but this sentence deviates from the main idea the most.

## 10. D

The following sentence, if inserted after sentence 11, "With the songs he composed, he established himself as an exemplary figure among fellow guitarists and the immediate generation that followed" best illustrates the main idea of the passage.

This sentence best complements the other sentences and the
main idea of the passage which concentrates on the impact
Alvin Lee has made on his admirers and contemporaries
with his skills and creations. The emphasis of the passage is
on how he influenced them with his guitar work and that is
complemented best if the sentence by choice D before sentence 11.

# VOCABULARY

|     | A | B | C | D | E |     | A | B | C | D | E |
|-----|---|---|---|---|---|-----|---|---|---|---|---|
| 1   | ○ | ○ | ○ | ○ | ○ | 21  | ○ | ○ | ○ | ○ | ○ |
| 2   | ○ | ○ | ○ | ○ | ○ | 22  | ○ | ○ | ○ | ○ | ○ |
| 3   | ○ | ○ | ○ | ○ | ○ | 23  | ○ | ○ | ○ | ○ | ○ |
| 4   | ○ | ○ | ○ | ○ | ○ | 24  | ○ | ○ | ○ | ○ | ○ |
| 5   | ○ | ○ | ○ | ○ | ○ | 25  | ○ | ○ | ○ | ○ | ○ |
| 6   | ○ | ○ | ○ | ○ | ○ |
| 7   | ○ | ○ | ○ | ○ | ○ |
| 8   | ○ | ○ | ○ | ○ | ○ |
| 9   | ○ | ○ | ○ | ○ | ○ |
| 10  | ○ | ○ | ○ | ○ | ○ |
| 11  | ○ | ○ | ○ | ○ | ○ |
| 12  | ○ | ○ | ○ | ○ | ○ |
| 13  | ○ | ○ | ○ | ○ | ○ |
| 14  | ○ | ○ | ○ | ○ | ○ |
| 15  | ○ | ○ | ○ | ○ | ○ |
| 16  | ○ | ○ | ○ | ○ | ○ |
| 17  | ○ | ○ | ○ | ○ | ○ |
| 18  | ○ | ○ | ○ | ○ | ○ |
| 19  | ○ | ○ | ○ | ○ | ○ |
| 20  | ○ | ○ | ○ | ○ | ○ |

**1. Choose the noun that means, self evident or clear obvious truth.**

    a.  Truism

    b.  Catharsis

    c.  Libertine

    d.  Tractable

**2. Choose the best definition for: virago**

    a. A loud domineering woman

    b. A quiet woman

    c. A load domineering Man

    d. A quiet man

**3.  When Joe broke his _______ in a skiing accident, his entire leg was in a cast.**

    a. Ankle

    b. Humerus

    c. Wrist

    d. Femur

**4.  Select another word for the underlined word in the sentence below.**

**At first I thought she was very rude and boorish, but when I talked to her again she was very <u>genteel.</u>**

    a. Chivalrous

    b. Hilarious

    c. Civilized

    d. Governance

**5. Choose an adjective that means corrupted, impure.**

    a. Adulterate

    b. Harbor

    c. Infuriate

    d. Inculcate

**6. Select another word for the underlined word in the sentence below.**

**Her business success showed that she was very <u>shrewd</u>.**

    a. Slow

    b. Astute

    c. Ignorant

    d. Heinous

**7. Choose an adjective that means, beyond what is obvious or evident.**

    a. Ulterior

    b. Sybarite

    c. Torsion

    d. Trenchant

**8. Choose a noun that means, homeless child or stray.**

    a. Elegy

    b. Waif

    c. Martyr

    d. Palaver

**9. Select another word for the underlined word in the sentence below.**

**His inheritance was very large - a <u>princely</u> sum!**

    a. Minor

    b. Tolerable

    c. Large

    d. Pittance

**10. What is the best definition of deprecate?**

    a. Approve

    b. Indifference

    c. Disapprove

    d. None of the above

**11. Choose the best definition for succor.**

    a. To suck on

    b. To hate

    c. To like

    d. Give help or assistance

**12. Select the synonym of conspicuous.**

    a. Important

    b. Prominent

    c. Beautiful

    d. Convincing

**13. Select the noun that means eagerness and enthusiasm.**

    a. Alacrity

    b. Happiness

    c. Donator

    d. Marital

**14. After Lisa's aunt had her tenth child, Lisa found that she had more than twenty _________.**

    a. Uncles

    b. Friends

    c. Stepsisters

    d. Cousins

**15. Select the word that means benevolence.**

    a. Happiness

    b. Courage

    c. Kindness

    d. Loyalty

**16. Select the verb that means, to make less severe.**

    a. Suspense

    b. Alleviate

    c. Ingrate

    d. Action

**17. What is the name of one who gives a gift or who gives money to a charity organization?**

    a. Captain

    b. Benefactor

    c. Source

    d. Teacher

**18. What is another word for subordinate, or person of lesser rank or authority?**

    a.  Palliate

    b.  Plebeian

    c.  Underling

    d.  Expiate

**19. Choose the best definition of specious.**

    a. Logical

    b. Illogical

    c. Emotional

    d. 2 species

**20. Choose the best definition of proscribe.**

    a. Welcome

    b. Write a prescription

    c. Condemn

    d. Give a diagnosis

**21. When Craig's dog was struck by a car, he rushed his pet to the ______________.**

    a. Emergency room

    b. Doctor

    c. Veterinarian

    d. Podiatrist

**22. Choose the best definition of the underlined word. She never made a mistake - her performance was always <u>impeccable</u>.**

    a. Charming

    b. Flattering

    c. Perfect

    d. Impervious

**23. Select the synonym of boisterous.**

    a. Loud

    b. Soft

    c. Gentle

    d. Warm

**24. Select the adjective that means hidden, secret, disguised.**

    a. Accustomed

    b. Covert

    c. Hide

    d. Carriage

**25. Select the verb that means straightforward, open and sincere.**

     a. Lawful

     b. Candid

     c. True

     d. Lawful

# Answer Key

**1. A**
**Truism:** n. self-evident or clear, obvious, truth.

**2. A**
**Virago:** Given to undue belligerence or ill manner at the slightest provocation; a shrew, a termagant.

**3. D**
**Femur:** n. The bone of the thigh or upper hind limb, articulating at the hip and the knee.

**4. C**
**Genteel:** Polite and well-mannered. Stylish or elegant. Aristocratic

**5. A**
**Adulterate:** v. To render (something) poorer in quality by adding another substance, typically an inferior one.

**6. B**
**Shrewd:** showing clever resourcefulness in practical matters, artful, tricky or cunning, astute, streetwise, knowledgeable

**7. A**
**Ulterior:** adj. beyond what is obvious or evident.

**8. B**
**Waif:** n. homeless child or stray.

**9. C**
**Princely:** In the manner of a royal prince's conduct; large or grand.

**10. C**
**Deprecate:** v. To belittle or express disapproval of.

**11. D**
**Succor:** v. Aid, assistance or relief given to one in distress; ministration.

**12. B**
**Conspicuous:** adj. Standing out so as to be clearly visible..

**13. A**
**Alacrity:** adj. Eagerness; liveliness; enthusiasm.

**14. D**
**Cousins**

**15. C**
**Benevolent:**  adj. Well meaning and kindly.

**16. B**
**Alleviate:** v. To make less severe, as a pain or difficulty.

**17. B**
**Benefactor:** n. Somebody who gives one a gift. Usually refers to someone who gives money to a charity or another form of organization.

**18. C**
**Underling**: n. subordinate of lesser rank or authority.

**19. B**
**Specious:** adj. Seemingly well-reasoned or factual, but actually fallacious or insincere; strongly held but false.

**20. C**
**Proscribe:** v. Denounce or condemn.

**21. C**
**Veterinarian:** n. A person qualified to treat diseased or injured animals.

**22. C**
**Impeccable:** adj. Perfect, without faults, flaws or errors.

**23. A**
**Boisterous:** adj. Noisy, energetic, and cheerful; rowdy.

**24. B**
**Covert:** adj. Partially hidden, disguised, secret, surreptitious.

**25. B**
**Candid:** adj. Straightforward, open and sincere.

# HELP WITH READING COMPREHENSION

At first sight, reading comprehension tests look challenging especially if you are given long essays to answer only two to three questions. While reading, you might notice your attention wandering, or you may feel sleepy. Do not be discouraged because there are various tactics and long-range strategies that make comprehending even long, boring essays easier.

**Your friends before your foes.** It is always best to start with passages with familiar subjects rather than those with unfamiliar ones. This approach applies the same logic as tackling easy questions before hard ones. Skip passages that do not interest you and leave them for later.

Don't use 'special' reading techniques. This is not the time for speed-reading or anything like that – just plain ordinary reading – not too slow and not too fast.

**Read through the entire passage and the questions before you do anything.** Many students try reading the questions first and then looking for answers in the passage thinking this approach is more efficient. What these students do not realize is that it is often hard to navigate in unfamiliar roads. If you do not familiarize yourself with the passage first, looking for answers become not only time-consuming but also dangerous because you might miss the context of the answer you are looking for. If you read the questions first you will only confuse yourself and lose valuable time.

Familiarize yourself with reading comprehension questions. If you are familiar with the common types of reading questions, you are able to take note of important parts of the passage, saving time. There are six major kinds of reading questions.

- **Main Idea**- Questions that ask for the central thought or significance of the passage.

- **Specific Details** - Questions that asks for explicitly stated ideas.

- **Drawing Inferences** - Questions that ask for a logical extension of statements.

- **Tone or Attitude** - Questions that test your ability to sense the emotional state of the author.

- **Context Meaning** – Questions that ask for the meaning of a word depending on the context.

- **Technique** – Questions that ask for the method of organization or the writing style of the author.

**Read. Read. Read**. The best preparation for reading comprehension tests is always to read, read and read. If you are not used to reading lengthy passages, you will probably lose concentration. Increase your attention span by making a habit out of reading.  Read everyday and increase the time slowly each day.

Reading Comprehension tests become less daunting when you have trained yourself to read and understand fast. Always remember that it is easier to understand passages you are interested in. Do not read through passages hastily. Make mental notes of ideas you may be asked.

## Reading Strategy

When facing the reading comprehension section of a standardized test, you need a strategy to be successful. You want to keep several steps in mind:

- **First, make a note of the time and the number of sections.** Time your work accordingly. Typically, four to five minutes per section is sufficient. Second, read the directions for each selection thoroughly before beginning (and listen carefully to any additional verbal instructions, as they will often clarify obscure or confusing written guidelines). You must know exactly how to do what you're about to do!

- **Now you're ready to begin reading the selection.** Read the passage carefully, noting significant characters or events on scrap paper or underlining on the test sheet. Many students find making a basic list in the margins helpful. Quickly jot down or underline one-word summaries of characters, notable happenings, numbers, or key ideas. This will help retain information and focus wandering thoughts. Remember, however, that your goal is to find the information that answers the questions. Even if you find the passage interesting, stay on track.

- **Now read the question and all the choices.** Now you have read the passage, have a general idea of the main ideas, and have marked the important points. Read the question and all the choices. Never choose an answer without reading them all! Questions are often designed to confuse – stay focussed and clear. Usually the answer choices will focus on one or two facts or inferences from the passage. Keep these clear in your mind.

- **Search for the answer.** With a very general idea of what the different choices are, go back to the passage and scan for the relevant information. Watch for big words, unusual or unique words. These make your job easier as you can scan the text for the particular word.

- **Mark the Answer.** Now you have the key information the question is looking for. Go back to the question, quickly scan the choices and mark the correct one.

Typically, there will be several questions dealing with facts from the selection, a couple more inference questions dealing with logical consequences of those facts, and periodically an application-oriented question surfaces to force you to make connections with what you already know. Some students prefer to answer the questions as listed, and feel classifying the question and then ordering is wasting precious time. Other students prefer to answer the different types of questions in order of how easy or difficult they are. The choice is yours and do whatever works for you. If you want to try answering in order of difficulty, here is a recommended order, answer fact questions first; they're easily found within the passage. Tackle inference problems next, after re-reading the question(s) as many times as you need to. Application or 'best guess' questions usually take the longest, so, save them for last.

Use the practice tests to try out both ways of answering and see what works for you.

For more help with reading comprehension, see Multiple Choice Secrets at www.multiple-choice.ca

# MAIN IDEA AND SUPPORTING DETAILS

Identifying the main idea, topic and supporting details in a passage can feel like an overwhelming task.  The passages used for standardized tests can be boring and seem difficult - Test writers don't use interesting passages or ones that talk about things most people are  familiar with.  Despite these obstacles, all passages and paragraphs will have the information you need to answer the questions.

The topic of a passage or paragraph is its subject. It's the general idea and can be summed up in a word or short phrase.  Sometimes, there is a short description of the passage if it's taken from a longer work.  Make sure you read the description as it might state  the topic of the passage.  If not, read the passage and ask yourself, "Who, or what is this about?" For example:

Over the years, school uniforms have been hotly debated.  Arguments are made that students have the right to show individuality and express themselves by choosing their own clothes.  However, this brings up social and academic issues.  Some kids cannot afford to wear the clothes they like and might be bullied  by the "better dressed" students.  With attention drawn to clothes and the individual, students will lose focus on class work and the reason they are in school. School uniforms should be mandatory.

**Ask:**  What is this paragraph about?

**Topic:**  school uniforms

Once you have the topic, it's easier to find the main idea. The main idea is a specific statement telling what the writer wants you to  know. Writers usually state the main idea as a thesis statement. If you're looking for the main idea of a single paragraph, the main idea is called the topic sentence and will probably be the first or last sentence.  If you're looking for the main idea of an entire passage,  look for the thesis statement in either the first or last paragraph.  The main idea is usually restated in the conclusion. To find the main idea of a passage or paragraph, follow these steps:

1. Find the topic.

2. Ask yourself, "What point is the author trying to make about the topic?"

3. Create your own sentence summarizing the author's point.

4. Look in the text for the sentence closest in meaning to yours.

Look at the example paragraph again.  It's already established that the topic of the paragraph is school uniforms. What is the main idea/topic sentence?

**Ask:** "What point is the author trying to make about school uniforms?"

**Summary:**  Students should wear school uniforms.

**Topic sentence:**  School uniforms should be mandatory.

**Main Idea:** School uniforms should be mandatory.

Each paragraph offers supporting details to explain the main idea.  The details could be facts or reasons, but they will always answer a question about the main idea.  What? Where?  Why?  When?  How? How much/many? Look at the example paragraph again.  You'll notice that more than one sentence answers a question about the main idea.  These are the supporting details.

**Main Idea:** School uniforms should be mandatory.

**Ask:** Why?  Some kids cannot afford to wear clothes they like and could be bullied by the "better dressed" kids.  Supporting Detail

With attention drawn to clothes and the individual, Students will lose focus on class work and the reason they are in school.  Supporting Detail

What if the author doesn't state the main idea in a topic sentence? The passage will have an implied main idea. It's not as difficult to find as it might seem. Paragraphs are always organized around ideas.  To find an implied main idea, you need to know the topic and then find the relationship between the supporting details. Ask yourself, "What is the point the author is making about the relationship between the details?"

> Cocoa is what makes chocolate good for you. Chocolate comes in many varieties.  These delectable flavors include milk chocolate, dark chocolate, semi-sweet, and white chocolate.

**Ask:** What is this paragraph about?

**Topic:** Chocolate

**Ask:** What? Where? Why? When? How? How much/many?

**Supporting details**: Chocolate is good for you because it is made of cocoa, Chocolate is delicious, Chocolate comes in different delicious flavors

**Ask:** What is the relationship between the details and what is the author's point?

**Main Idea:** Chocolate is good because it is healthy and it tastes good.

# TESTING TIPS FOR MAIN IDEA QUESTIONS

1.  **Skim the questions** – not the answer choices - before reading the passage.

2. **Questions about main idea might use the words "theme," "generalization," or "purpose."**

3. **Save questions about the main idea for last.**  Questions can often be found in order in the passage.

3. **Underline topic sentences in the passage.**  Most tests allow you to write in your test booklet.

4. **Answer the question in your own words before looking at the answer choices.** Then match your answer with an answer choice.

5. **Cross out incorrect answer choices immediately to prevent confusion.**

6. **If two of the answer choices mean the same thing but use different words, they are BOTH incorrect.**

7. **If a question asks about the whole passage, cross out the answer choices that apply to only part of it.**

**8. If only part of the information is correct, that answer choice is incorrect.**

**9. An answer choice that is too broad is incorrect.** All information needs to be backed up by the passage.

**10. Answer choices with extreme wording are usually incorrect. What is most likely Shelly's job?**

    a. Musician

    b. Lawyer

    c. Doctor

    d. Teacher

# HELP WITH BUILDING YOUR VOCABULARY

Vocabulary tests can be daunting when you think of the enormous number of words that might come up in the exam. As the exam date draws near, your anxiety will grow because you know that no matter how many words you memorize, chances are, you will still remember so few. Here are some tips which you can use to hurdle the big words that may come up in your exam without having to open the dictionary and memorize all the words known to humankind.

Build up and tear apart the big words. Big words, like many other things, are composed of small parts. Some words are made up of many other words. A man who lifts weights for example, is a weight lifter. Words are also made up of word parts called prefixes, suffixes and roots. Often times, we can see the relationship of different words through these parts. A person who is skilled with both hands is ambidextrous. A word with double meaning is ambiguous. A person with two conflicting emotions is ambivalent. Two words with synonymous meanings often have the same root. Bio, a root word derived from Latin is used in words like biography meaning to write about a person's life, and biology meaning the study of living organisms.

- **Words with double meanings.** Did you know that the word husband not only means a man married to a woman, but also thrift or frugality? Sometimes, words have double meanings. The dictionary meaning, or the denotation of a word is sometimes different from the way we use it or its connotation.

- **Read widely, read deeply and read daily.** The best way to expand your vocabulary is to familiarize yourself with as many words as possible through reading. By reading, you are able to remember words in a proper context and thus, remember its meaning or at the very least, its use. Reading widely would help you get acquainted with words you may never use every day. This is the best strategy without doubt. However, if you are studying for an exam next week, or even tomorrow, it isn't much help! Below you will find a range of different ways to learn new words quickly and efficiently.

- **Remember.** Always remember that big words are easy to understand when divided into smaller parts, and the smaller words will often have several other meanings aside from the one you already know. Below is an extensive list of root or stem words, followed by one hundred questions to help you learn word stems.

Here are suggested effective ways to help you improve your vocabulary.

**Be Committed To Learning New Words**. To improve your vocabulary you need to make a commitment to learn new words. Commit to learning at least a word or two a day. You can also get new words by reading books, poems, stories, plays and magazines. Expose yourself to more language to increase the number of new words that you learn.

- **Learn Practical Vocabulary**. As much as possible, learn vocabulary that is associated with what you do and that you can use regularly. For example learn words related to your profession or hobby. Learn as much vocabulary as you can in your favorite subjects.

- **Use New Words Frequently**. When you learn a new word start using it and do so frequently. Repeat it when you are alone and try to use the word as often as you can with people you talk to. You can also use flash-cards to practice new words that you learn.

• **Learn the Proper Usage.** If you do not understand the proper usage, look it up and make sure you have it right.

• **Use a Dictionary**. When reading textbooks, novels or assigned readings, keep the dictionary nearby. Also learn how to use online dictionaries and WORD dictionary. When you come across a new word, check for its meaning. If you cannot do so immediately, then you should write it down and check it when possible. This will help you understand what the word means and exactly how best to use it.

• **Learn Word Roots, Prefixes and Suffixes.** English words are usually derived from suffixes, prefixes and roots, which come from Latin, French or Greek. Learning the root or origin of a word helps you easily understand the meaning of the word and other words that are derived from the root. Generally, if you learn the meaning of one root word, you will understand two or three words. See our List of Stem Words below.  This is a great two-for-one strategy. Most prefixes, suffixes, roots and stems are used in two, three or more words, so if you know the root, prefix or suffix, you can guess the meaning of many words.

• **Synonyms and Antonyms**. Most words in the English language have two or three (at least) synonyms and antonyms. For example, "big," in the most common usage, has about seventy-five synonyms and an equal number of antonyms. Understanding the relationships between these words and how they all fit together gives your brain a framework, which makes them easier to learn, remember and recall.

• **Use Flash Cards**. Flash cards are one of the best ways to memorize things. They can be used anywhere and anytime, so you can make use of odd free moments waiting for the bus or waiting in line. Make your own or buy commercially prepared flash cards, and keep them with you all the time.

- **Make word lists.** Learning vocabulary, like learning many things, requires repetition. Keep a new words journal in a separate section or separate notebook. Add any words that you look up in the dictionary, as well as from word lists. Review your word lists regularly.

Photocopying or printing off word lists from the Internet or handouts is not the same. Actually writing out the word and a few notes on the definition is an important process for imprinting the word in your brain. Writing out the word and definition in your New Word Journal, forces you to concentrate and focus on the new word. Hitting PRINT or pushing the button on the photocopier does not do the same thing.

Notice the verbs in bold in the examples above. They are encircling the subjects of each sentence rather than following them. This is inverse word order.

# English Grammar and Usage

|    | A | B | C | D | E |     | A | B | C | D | E |
|----|---|---|---|---|---|-----|---|---|---|---|---|
| 1  | ○ | ○ | ○ | ○ | ○ | 21  | ○ | ○ | ○ | ○ | ○ |
| 2  | ○ | ○ | ○ | ○ | ○ | 22  | ○ | ○ | ○ | ○ | ○ |
| 3  | ○ | ○ | ○ | ○ | ○ | 23  | ○ | ○ | ○ | ○ | ○ |
| 4  | ○ | ○ | ○ | ○ | ○ | 24  | ○ | ○ | ○ | ○ | ○ |
| 5  | ○ | ○ | ○ | ○ | ○ | 25  | ○ | ○ | ○ | ○ | ○ |
| 6  | ○ | ○ | ○ | ○ | ○ |     |   |   |   |   |   |
| 7  | ○ | ○ | ○ | ○ | ○ |     |   |   |   |   |   |
| 8  | ○ | ○ | ○ | ○ | ○ |     |   |   |   |   |   |
| 9  | ○ | ○ | ○ | ○ | ○ |     |   |   |   |   |   |
| 10 | ○ | ○ | ○ | ○ | ○ |     |   |   |   |   |   |
| 11 | ○ | ○ | ○ | ○ | ○ |     |   |   |   |   |   |
| 12 | ○ | ○ | ○ | ○ | ○ |     |   |   |   |   |   |
| 13 | ○ | ○ | ○ | ○ | ○ |     |   |   |   |   |   |
| 14 | ○ | ○ | ○ | ○ | ○ |     |   |   |   |   |   |
| 15 | ○ | ○ | ○ | ○ | ○ |     |   |   |   |   |   |
| 16 | ○ | ○ | ○ | ○ | ○ |     |   |   |   |   |   |
| 17 | ○ | ○ | ○ | ○ | ○ |     |   |   |   |   |   |
| 18 | ○ | ○ | ○ | ○ | ○ |     |   |   |   |   |   |
| 19 | ○ | ○ | ○ | ○ | ○ |     |   |   |   |   |   |
| 20 | ○ | ○ | ○ | ○ | ○ |     |   |   |   |   |   |

## Part 1 - Punctuation

**1. Ted and Janice <u>who had been friends for years went on vacation together</u> every summer.**

    a. Ted and Janice, who had been friends for years, went on vacation together every summer.

    b. Ted and Janice who had been friends for years, went on vacation together every summer.

    c. Ted, and Janice who had been friends for years, went on vacation together every summer.

    d. None of the choices are correct.

**2. None of us want to go to the <u>party not even</u> if there will be live music.**

    a. None of us want to go to the party not even, if there will be live music.

    b. None of us want to go to the party, not even if there will be live music.

    c. None of us want to go to the party; not even if there will be live music.

    d. None of the choice are correct.

**3. <u>John, Maurice, and Thomas,</u> quit school two months before graduation.**

    a. John, Maurice, and Thomas quit school two months before graduation.

    b. John, Maurice and Thomas quit school two months before graduation.

    c. John Maurice and Thomas, quit school two months before graduation.

    d. None of the choice are correct.

**4. "My father said that he would be there on <u>Sunday,"</u> <u>Lee</u> explained.**

    a. "My father said that he would be there on Sunday" Lee explained.

    b. None of the choices are correct.

    c. "My father said that he would be there on Sunday," Lee explained.

    d. "My father said that he would be there on Sunday." Lee explained.

**5. I own two <u>dogs, a cat, named Jeffrey and Henry, the</u> <u>goldfish.</u>**

    a. I own two dogs, a cat named Jeffrey, and Henry, the goldfish.

    b. I own two dogs  a cat, named Jeffrey, and Henry, the goldfish.

    c. I own two dogs, a cat named Jeffrey; and Henry, the goldfish.

    d. None of the choices are correct.

**6. Choose the sentence below with the correct punctuation.**

    a.   Marcus who won the debate tournament, is the best speaker that I know.

    b.   Marcus, who won the debate tournament, is the best speaker that I know.

    c.   Marcus who won the debate tournament is the best speaker that I know.

    d.   Marcus who won the debate tournament is the best speaker, that I know.

# PART II - SENTENCE STRUCTURE AND GRAMMAR

**Combine the sentences below into one sentence with the same meaning.**

**7. I hate needles.  I want to give blood.  I can't give blood.**

    a.  Although I hate needles, I couldn't give blood even if I wanted to.
    b.  Because I hate needles, I can't give blood, although I want to give blood.
    c.  Whenever I hate needles, I give blood although I can't give blood.
    d.  Whenever I can't give blood, I give blood anyway, although I hate needles.

**8.  The doctor was not looking forward to meeting Mrs. Lucas.  The doctor would have to tell Mrs. Lucas that she has cancer.  The doctor hates giving bad news to patients.**

a. The doctor hates giving bad news, so he was not looking forward to meeting Mrs. Lucas and telling her she has cancer.

b. The doctor has cancer and was not looking forward to meeting Mrs. Lucas and telling her the bad news.

c. Before the doctor met Mrs. Lucas, he had to give his the patients the bad news that Mrs. Lucas has cancer.

d. The doctor was not looking forward to giving the bad news to his patients that he had to tell Mrs. Lucas that his patients have cancer.

**9. Mom hates shopping.  We were out of bread, milk and eggs.  Mom went to the supermarket.**

> a. Because we were out of bread, milk and eggs, Mom hated shopping at the supermarket.
> b. Although she hates shopping, Mom went to the supermarket since we were out of bread, milk and eggs.
> c. Although we were out of bread, milk and eggs, Mom still hated shopping at the supermarket and went there anyway.
> d. Because Mom hated shopping at the supermarket, she went to there to buy her bread, milk and eggs.

**10. The ceremony had an emotional <u>affect</u> on the groom, but the bride was not <u>affected</u>.**

> a. The ceremony had an emotional effect on the groom, but the bride was not affected.
>
> b. The ceremony had an emotional affect on the groom, but the bride was not affected.
>
> c. The ceremony had an emotional effect on the groom, but the bride was not effected.

**11. Anna was taller <u>than Luis, but then</u> he grew four inches in three months.**

> a.  None of the choices are correct.
> b.  Anna was taller then Luis, but than he grew four inches in three months.
> c.  Anna was taller than Luis, but than he grew four inches, in three months.
> d.  Anna was taller than Luis, but then he grew four inches in three months.

**12.  <u>There</u> second home is in Boca Raton, but <u>they're</u> not <u>there</u> for most of the year.**

    a. Their second home is in Boca Raton, but there not their for most of the year.

    b. They're second home is in Boca Raton, but they're not there for most of the year.

    c. Their second home is in Boca Raton, but they're not there for most of the year.

    d. None of the choices are correct.

**13. <u>Their</u> going to graduate in June; after that, <u>their</u> best option will be to go <u>there.</u>**

    a. They're going to graduate in June; after that, their best option will be to go there.

    b. There going to graduate in June; after that, their best option will be to go there.

    c. They're going to graduate in June; after that, there best option will be to go their.

    d. None of the choices are correct.

**14. Your mistaken; that is not you're book.**

    a. You're mistaken; that is not you're book.

    b. Your mistaken; that is not your book.

    c. You're mistaken; that is not your book.

    d. None of the choices are correct.

**15. <u>You're</u> classes are on the west side of campus, but <u>you're</u> living on the east side.**

    a. You're classes are on the west side of campus, but you're living on the east side.

    b. Your classes are on the west side of campus, but your living on the east side.

    c. Your classes are on the west side of campus, but you're living on the east side.

    d. None of the choices are correct.

**16. The Chinese lives in one of the world's most populous nations, while a citizen of Bermuda lives in one of the least populous.**

    a. The Chinese live in one of the world's most populous nations, while a citizen of Bermuda lives in one of the least populous.

    b. The Chinese lives in one of the world's most populous nations, while a citizen of Bermuda live in one of the least populous.

    c. The Chinese live in one of the world's most populous nations, while a citizen of Bermuda live in one of the least populous.

    d. None of the choices are correct.

**17. You shouldn't <u>sit</u> in that chair wearing black pants; I <u>sit</u> the white cat there just a moment ago.**

    a. You shouldn't sit in that chair wearing black pants; I set the white cat there just a moment ago.

    b. You shouldn't set in that chair wearing black pants; I sit the white cat there just a moment ago.

    c. You shouldn't set in that chair wearing black pants; I set the white cat there just a moment ago.

    d. None of the choices are correct.

**18. We saw the <u>golden gate Bridge in San Francisco.</u>**

    a. Golden Gate Bridge in San Francisco

    b. golden gate bridge in San Francisco

    c. Golden gate bridge in San Francisco

    d. None of the choice are correct.

# PART III - SENTENCE COMPLETION AND CORRECTION

**19. Collecting stamps, ____________________ and listening to shortwave radio were Rick's main hobbies.**

    a. building models
    b.  to build models
    c. having built models
    d. build models

**20. Every morning, _______, and before the sun comes up, my mother makes herself a cup of cocoa.**

    a. after the kids left for school
    b.  after the kids leave for school
    c. after the kids have left for school
    d. after the kids will leave for school

**21. Elaine promised to bring the camera ________________ at the mall yesterday.**

    a. by me
    b.  with me
    c. at me
    d. to me

**22. Following the tornado, telephone poles __________ all over the street.**

   a. laid
   b. lied
   c. were lying
   d. were laying

**Part IV - Grammar – Sentence Correction**

**23. She is the <u>most cleverest</u> girl in the class.**

   a.   She is the most clever girl in the class.
   b.   She is the cleverest girl in the class.
   c.   She is the most cleverer girl in the class.
   d.   None of the above.

**24. He <u>lived</u> in California since 1995.**

   a.   He had lived in California since 1995.
   b.   He has been living in California since 1995.
   c.   He has living in California since 1995.
   d.   None of the above.

**25. Please excuse <u>me being</u> late.**

   a.   Please excuse me for late.
   b.   Please excuse my being late.
   c.   Please excuse my being lateness.
   d.   None of the above.

# Answer Key

**1. A**

Use a comma to separate phrases.

**2. B**

Use a comma separates independent clauses.  None of us wants to go to the party, not even if there will be live music.

**3. B**

Don't use a comma before 'and' in a list.

**4. C**

Commas always go with a quote and the use of said, explained etc.

**5. A**

This is an example if a comma which appears before 'and,' but is disambiguating.  Without the comma, the sentence would be "I own two dogs, a cat named Jeffrey and Henry, the goldfish."  This means there is a cat named Jeffrey and Henry, and a goldfish with no name mentioned.   The comma appears to show the distinction.

I own two dogs, a cat named Jeffrey, and Henry, the goldfish.

**6. B**

Comma separate phrases.

**7. A**

These three sentences can be combined using 'although,' and 'even if.'

**8. A**

These two sentences can be combined into one sentence with two clauses separated by a comma.

**9. B**

These three sentences can be combined using 'although,' and 'since.'

# English Usage

### 10.  A
Affect vs. Effect - Affect is a verb (action) and effect is a noun (thing).

### 11.  D
Than vs. Then – Than is used for comparison, as in, taller than, and then is used for time, as in, but then...

### 12. C
There vs. their vs. they're.  There indicates existence as in, "there are."  Their is to indicate possession, as in, "their book."  They're is the contraction form of "they are."

### 13.  A
There vs. their vs. they're.  There indicates existence as in, "there are."  Their is to indicate possession, as in, "their book."  They're is the contraction form of "they are."

### 14. C
Your vs. you're.  Your is the possessive form of you.  You're is the contraction form of you are.

### 15. C
Your vs. you're.  Your is the possessive form of you.  You're is the contraction form of you are.

### 16. A
Singular subjects.  "The Chinese" is plural, and "a citizen of Bermuda" is singular.

### 17. A
Sit vs. Set.  Set requires an object – something to set down.  Sit is something that you do, like sit on the chair.

### 18. A
Always capitalize proper nouns.

### 19. A
Present progressive "building models" is correct in this sentence.

### 20. C
Past Perfect tense describes a completed action in the past, before another action in the past.

### 21. D
The preposition 'to' in this sentence means give.

### 22. C
"Lie" means to recline, and does not take an object.  'Lay' means to place and does take an object. Peter lay the books on the table, or the telephone poles were lying on the road.

### 23. B
Cleverest is the proper form to express 'most clever.'

### 24. B
Past perfect continuous, has been living, is proper because the time element, since 1995, and he is still living there now.

### 25. B
The correct form is, "please excuse me for being late," or, "please excuse my being late."

# English Grammar and Punctuation Tutorials

## Capitalization

Although many of the rules for capitalization are pretty straight forward, there are several tricky points that are important to review.

### Starting a Sentence

Everyone knows that you need to capitalize the first letter of the first word in a sentence, but is it really all that easy to figure out where one sentence starts and another stops? Take these three examples:

That was the moment it really sunk in: There would be no hockey this year.

It was April and that could mean only one thing: baseball.

We played for hours before heading home; everyone felt tired and happy.

In the first example, the first letter after the colon is capitalized while in the second example, it is not. That is because everything after the first example's colon is a complete sentence, while example two's colon there is only one word. In example three you have what could be a complete sentence ("everyone felt tired and happy"), but which is not because it follows a semicolon, making it just another clause instead.

Within a sentence you can have an additional complete sentence if the sentence follows a colon. However, if what could be a complete sentence follows a semicolon, it is a clause and does not get capitalized.

Remember that the same rules apply for quotation marks that apply for colons: A complete sentence inside quotation marks is capitalized, but a single word or phrase is not.

## Proper Nouns

The first letter of all proper nouns needs to be capitalized. There are many categories of proper noun. The most common proper nouns are the specific names of people (such as Bill), places (such as Germany) or things (such as Honda Civic). However, there are several less obvious categories of words that should be capitalized as proper nouns.

Historical events such as World War II or the California Gold Rush need to be capitalized.

The names of celestial bodies such as Orion's Belt need to be capitalized.

The names of ethnicities such as African-American or Hispanic need to be capitalized.

Relationship words that replace a person's name such as Mom, Doctor and Mister need to be capitalized. However, this only happens when you use the word to replace the person's name. In the sentence, "My mom went to the store," you do not capitalize it, while in the sentence, "Hey Mom, did you get toothpaste at the store?" you do capitalize it.

Geographical locations are capitalized. This can be tricky because capitalized geographical locations and non-capitalized directions are easy to confuse. Saying, "We drove south for hours," is a direction, so the word "south" should not be capitalized. However, when saying, "While in the United States, we drove to the South to look at Civil War battle fields," you do capitalize the word "South." The difference is that in the first sentence "south" is just the direction you drove. In the second sentence "the South" is a specific region of the United States that formed itself into the Confederacy during the US Civil War.

## Proper Adjectives

Proper adjectives are the adjective forms of proper nouns. People from Germany are German; people from Canada are Canadian. German and Canadian are proper adjectives because they are forms of proper nouns that are used to describe other nouns.

### Titles of Works

Titles of works are generally capitalized following a specific pattern. Capitalize all the important words in a sentence. Do not capitalize unimportant words such as prepositions and articles.

For example: Alien Spaceship Spotted over Many of the World's Capitals

Notice that the prepositions "over" and "of," and the article "the" are the only non-capitalized words in the sentence.

# PUNCTUATION – COLONS, SEMICOLONS, HYPHENS, DASHES, PARENTHESES AND APOSTROPHES

Within a sentence there are several different types of punctuation marks that can denote a pause. Each of these punctuation marks has different rules when it comes to its structure and usage, so we will look at each one in turn.

### Colons

The colon is used primarily to introduce information. It can start lists such as in the sentence, "There were several things Susan had to get at the store: bread, cereal, lettuce and tomatoes." Or a colon points out specific information, such as in the sentence, "It was only then that the group fully realized what had happened: The Martian invasion had begun."

Note that if the information after the colon is a complete sentence, you capitalize and punctuate it exactly like you would a sentence. If, however, it does not constitute a complete sentence, you don't have to capitalize anything. ("Peering out the window Meredith saw them: zombies.")

## SEMICOLONS

Semicolons are super commas. They denote a stronger stop than a comma does, but they are still weaker than a period, not capable of ending a sentence. Semicolons are primarily used to separate independent clauses that are not being separated by a coordinating conjunction. ("Chris went to the store; he bought chips and salsa.") Semicolons can only do this, however, when the ideas in each clause are related. For instance, the sentence, "It's raining outside; my sister went to the movies," is not a proper usage of the semicolon since those clauses have nothing to do with each other.

Semicolons can also be used in lists if one or more element in the list is itself made up of a smaller list. If you want to write a list of things you plan to bring to a picnic, and those things only include a Frisbee, a chair and some pasta salad, you would not need to use a semicolon. However, if you also wanted to bring plastic knives, forks and spoons, you would need to write your sentence like this: "For our picnic I am bringing a Frisbee; a chair; plastic knives, forks and spoons; and some pasta salad."

Using semicolons like this preserves the smaller list that you have in your larger list.

## HYPHENS

To join words together to show that they are linked you use hyphens. The most common use of hyphens is to link together words to show that they are working together in a sentence. ("The well-known actor was eating at the table behind us.") This shows explicitly that you are using "well-known" as a single concept and not as two descriptive words in a list.

Hyphens can also be used to split a word in half if you run out of space writing on one line of a page. This is often seen in newspapers and magazines when text is justified to both sides of a page or a column. For example:

The massive earthquake caused surpris-

ingly little damage in the affected areas.

However, you can only use a hyphen in this way if you split the word between syllables. Often students think that they can use hyphens to break up words wherever they want; this is wrong. For the word "surprisingly" you could have a hyphen between "sur" and "prisingly," "surpris" and "ingly, and between "surprising" and "ly," but nowhere else.

Finally, hyphens can be used to add prefixes to words. This happens a lot in news reports with phrases such as "pro-government troops."

Dashes and Parentheses

Both dashes and parentheses are used to set aside information into parenthetical statements; statements that can be treated as an aside. They do not need to be there for the sentence to make sense, but the information they provide is interesting enough that you feel it should be included. Parentheses are considered stronger than dashes are. (Commas can also be used to separate nonessential information from a sentence, but they are considered to be the weakest of the three.)

As the previous sentence shows, parentheses can surround entire sentences, separating them from the paragraph. Dashes, on the other hand, can separate off the last statement in a sentence. ("Calvin came home and greeted his family for the first time in days—everyone smiled.") Obviously, that last sentence could also be written using a semicolon or as two sentences. The difference is in how you want it to sound to the reader. Should these thoughts be treated as two distinct pieces? Or should everyone smiling at Calvin be part of the main sentence, just separated a bit more strongly—with a slightly longer pause—than a comma could manage?

## APOSTROPHES

There are two primary uses of the apostrophe in English: forming contractions and forming possessive nouns.

Contractions are formed by taking two words and combining them together with an apostrophe replacing the missing letters (do not becomes don't), or by shortening an existing word (cannot becomes can't). Apostrophes can

also make contractions by attaching verbs to nouns or pronouns. ("He's going to the store.")

When making singular nouns possessive the general rule is that you add an 's to the end of singular nouns. (This is Tim's bagel.) When dealing with plural nouns that do not end with the letter –s (such as children), the rule is that you also add an 's to the end of the word. (It was the children's favorite movie.) And when dealing with plural nouns that end with the letter –s, you simply add an apostrophe. (My sisters' favorite game is tag.)

However, and this is an important "however" given the controversy it can cause, when dealing with singular words that end with the letter –s (such as circus), there are two standards for how to make them possessive—each with its own grammar books to back it up.

One standard says that you still add an 's to the end of the word. (This is the circus's biggest tent.) The other says that, since the word ends with an –s, it can only get an apostrophe. (This is the circus' biggest tent.) Some style books, such as the Chicago Manual of Style will go so far as to say that the former option is correct, but to avoid inflaming people's passions on the subject, using the latter is perfectly acceptable. The best thing to do is to find out which style the teacher or editor you are writing for at any given time prefers and conform to it for that person.

# Commas

Commas are probably the most commonly used punctuation mark in English. Commas can break the flow of writing to give it a more natural sounding style, and they are the main punctuation mark used to separate ideas. Commas also separate lists, introductory adverbs, introductory prepositional phrases, dates and addresses.

The most rigid way that commas are used is when separating clauses. There are two primary types of clauses in a sentence, independent and subordinate (sometimes called dependent). Independent clauses are clauses that express a complete thought, such as, "Tim went to the store." Subordinate clauses, on the other hand, only express partial thoughts that expand on an independent clause, such as, "after the game ended," which you can see is clearly not a complete sentence. (You will learn more about clauses in different lessons.)

The rule for commas with clauses is that a comma must separate the clauses when a subordinate clause comes first in a sentence: "After the game ended, Tim went to the store." But there should not be a comma when a subordinate clause follows an independent clause: "Tim went to the store after the game ended." If you leave the comma out of the first example, you have a run-on sentence. If you add one into the second example, you have a comma-splice error. Also, when you have two independent clauses joined with a coordinating conjunction, you need to separate them with a comma. "Tim went to the store, and Beth went home."

There are some artistic exceptions to these rules, such as adding a pause for literary effect, but for the most part, they are set in stone.

Commas are also used to separate items in a list. This area of English is unfortunately less clear than it should be, with two separate rules depending on what standard you are following. To understand the two different rules, let's pretend you are having a party at your house, and you are making a list of refreshments your friends will want. You may decide to serve three things: 1) pizza 2) chips 3) drinks. There are two different rules governing how you should punctuate this. According to many grammar books, you would write this as, "At the store I will buy pizza, chips, and drinks." This variation puts a comma after each item in the list. It is the version that the style books used in most college English and history courses will prefer, so it is probably the one you should follow. However, the Associated Press style guide, which is used in college journalism classes and at newspapers and magazines, says the sentence should be written like this: "At the store I will buy pizza, chips and drinks." Here you only use a comma between the first two words, letting the word "and" act as the separator between the last two.

Another important place to use commas is when you have a modifier that describes an element of a sentence, but that does not directly follow the thing it describes. Look at the sentence: "Tim went over to visit Beth, watching the full moon along the way." In this sentence there is no confusion about who is "watching the full moon"; it is Tim, probably as he walks to Beth's house. If you remove the comma, however, you get this: "Tim went over to visit Beth watching the full moon along the way." Now it sounds as though Beth is watching the full moon, and we are forced to wonder what "way" the moon is traveling along.

Commas are also used when adding introductory prepositional phrases and introductory adverbs to sentences. A comma is always needed following an introductory adverb. ("Quickly, Jody ran to the car.") Commas are even necessary when you have an adverb introducing a clause within a sentence, even if the clause not the first clause of the sentence. ("Amanda wanted to go to the movie; however, she knew her homework was more important.")

With introductory prepositional phrases you only add a comma if the phrase (or if a group of introductory phrases) is five or more words long. Thus, the sentence you just read did not have a comma following its introductory prepositional phrase ("With introductory prepositional phrases") because it was only four words. Compare that to this sentence with a five word introductory phrase: "After the ridiculously long class, the friends needed to relax."

The last main way that commas are used in sentences is to separate out information that does not need to be there. For instance, "My cousin Hector, who wore a blue hat at the party, thought you were funny." The fact that Hector wore a blue hat is interesting, but it is not vital to the sentence; it could be removed and not changed the sentence's meaning. Therefore it gets commas around it. Along these lines you should remember that any clause introduced by the word that is considered to provide essential information to the sentence and should not get commas around it. Conversely, any clause starting with the word which is considered non-essential and should not get commas around it.

# Quotation Marks

Quotation marks are used in English in a variety of different ways. The most common use of quotation marks is to show quotations either as dialogue or when directly quoting a source in an essay or news article. Fortunately, both of these uses follow the same basic rules.

When you have a quote written as the second part of a sentence, you need to put a comma before the quotation marks and a period inside the quotation marks at the end. (Franklin said, "Let's go to the store.") Conversely, when you have quote as the first part of the sentence with information describing it second, a comma replaces the period at the end of the sentence inside the quotes. ("Let's go to the store," Franklin said.)

If the information in a quote is not a complete sentence, you do not need to capitalize it or put commas around it, if it is not dialogue. (No one thought the idea of "going to the store" sounded very fun.)

Note that when the last word in a sentence has both a quotation mark and a period attached to it, the period is always inside the quotes. This is the case when you have a complete sentence inside a quote ("Let's go to the store."), and when the last word in a sentence just happens to have quote marks around it (Kerri said I was "mean.") You also need to do the same thing with commas. (Kerri said I was "mean," and it made me feel bad.) However, other punctuation marks such as colons, semicolons and dashes do not follow this rule and should come outside the quotes. (Kerri said I was "mean"; it made me feel bad.)

When you want to use a quote inside a quote, you use the standard double-quotation marks for the outer quote and single-quotation marks for the inner quote. ("The sign on the door said 'no soliciting,' so we went to the next house.")

Quotation marks are also used around certain types of titles. To figure out which ones, it helps to look at which titles are not put in quotes as well.

Titles have two categories: large works and small works. Large works are things such as newspapers, magazines, CDs, books and television shows. The defining character- istic of a large work is that it is able to hold small works in it. Small works are the articles inside newspapers and magazines, the songs on a CD, the chapters in a book and the episodes of a television show. It is small works that get quotation marks around them. (Large works, meanwhile, are either underlined or italicized.)

Using quotation marks correctly in a title looks something like this: The two-page article entitled "San Francisco Giants Win World Series" appeared in yesterday's New York Times. The article title is in quotes, and the newspaper title is in italics.

# SUBJECT VERB AGREEMENT

Verbs in any sentence must agree with the subject of the sentence in person and number. Problems usually occur when the verb doesn't correspond with the right subject or the verb fails to match the noun close to it.

Unfortunately, there is no easy way around these principals - no tricky strategy or easy rule.   You just have to memorize them.

Here is a quick review:

The verb to be, present (past)

| PERSON | SINGULAR | PLURAL |
|---|---|---|
| First | I am (was) | we are (were) |
| Second | you are (were) | you are (were) |
| Third | he, she, it is (was) | they are (were) |

The verb to have, present (past)

| PERSON | SINGULAR | PLURAL |
|---|---|---|
| First | I have (had) | we have (had) |
| Second | you have (had) | you have (had) |
| Third | he, she, it has (had) | they have (had) |

Regular verbs, e.g. to walk, present (past)

| PERSON | SINGULAR | PLURAL |
|---|---|---|
| First | I walk (walked) | we walk (walked) |
| Second | you walk (walked) | you walk (walked) |
| Third | he, she, it walks (walked) | they work (walked) |

## 1. EVERY AND EACH

When nouns are qualified by "every" or "each," they take a singular verb even if they are joined by 'and'

**Examples:**

Each mother and daughter *was* a given separate test.
Every teacher and student *was* properly welcomed.

## 2. PLURAL NOUNS

Nouns like measles, tongs, trousers, riches, scissors etc. are all plural.

**Examples:**

The trousers *are* dirty.
My scissors *have* gone missing.
The tongs *are* on the table.

## 3. WITH AND AS WELL

Two subjects linked by "with" or "as well" should have a verb that matches the first subject.

**Examples:**

The pencil, with the papers and equipment, *is* on the desk.
David as well as Louis is coming.

## 4. PLURAL NOUNS

The following nouns take a singular verb:

politics, mathematics, innings, news, advice, summons, furniture, information, poetry, machinery, vacation, scenery

**Examples:**

The machinery *is* difficult to assemble
The furniture *has* been delivered
The scenery *was* beautiful

## 5. SINGLE ENTITIES

A proper noun in plural form that refers to a single entity requires a singular verb. This is a complicated way of saying; some things appear to be plural, but are really singular, or some nouns refer to a collection of things but the collection is really singular.

**Examples:**

The United Nations Organization *is* the decision maker in the matter.

Here the "United Nations Organization" is really only one "thing" or noun, but is made up of many "nations."

The book, "The Seven Virgins" *was* not available in the library.

Here there is only one book, although the title of the book is plural.

# 6. SPECIFIC AMOUNTS ARE ALWAYS SINGULAR

A plural noun that refers to a specific amount or quantity that is considered as a whole (dozen, hundred, score etc.) requires a singular verb.

**Examples:**

60 minutes *is* quite a long time.
Here "60 minutes" is considered a whole, and therefore one item (singular noun).
The first million is the most difficult.

# 7. EITHER, NEITHER AND EACH ARE ALWAYS SINGULAR

The verb is always singular when used with: either, each, neither, every one and many.

**Examples:**

*Either* of the boys *is* lying.
*Each* of the employees *has* been well compensated

*Many* a police officer *has* been found to be courageous
*Every one* of the teachers *is* responsible

## 8. LINKING WITH EITHER, OR, AND NEITHER MATCH THE SECOND SUBJECT

Two subjects linked by "either," "or,""nor" or "neither" should have a verb that matches the second subject.

**Examples:**

*Neither* David nor Paul *will* be coming.
*Either* Mary or Tina *is* paying.
**Note**
If one subject linked by "either," "or,""nor" or "neither" is in plural form, then the verb should also be in plural, and the verb should be close to the plural subject.

**Examples:**
*Neither* the mother *nor* her kids *have* eaten.
Either Mary *or* her *friends are* paying.

## 9. COLLECTIVE NOUNS ARE PLURAL

Some collective nouns such as poultry, gentry, cattle, vermin etc. are considered plural and require a plural verb.

**Examples:**

The *poultry are* sick.
The *cattle are* well fed.

**Note**
Collective nouns involving people can work with both plural and singular verbs.

**Examples:**

Nigerians are known to be hard working
Europeans live in Africa

# 10. NOUNS THAT ARE SINGULAR AND PLURAL

Nouns like deer, sheep, swine, salmon etc. can be singular or plural and require the same verb form.

**Examples:**

The swine is feeding. (singular)
The swine are feeding. (plural)

The salmon is on the table. (singular)
The salmon are running upstream.  (plural)

# 11. COLLECTIVE NOUNS ARE SINGULAR

Collective nouns such as Army, Jury, Assembly, Committee, Team etc should carry a singular verb when they subscribe to one idea. If the ideas or views are more than one, then the verb used should be plural.

**Examples:**

The committee is in agreement in their decision.

The committee were in disagreement in their decision.
The jury has agreed on a verdict.
The jury were unable to agree on a verdict.

# 12. SUBJECTS LINKS BY "AND" ARE PLURAL.

Two subjects linked by "and" always require a plural verb

**Examples:**

David and John are students.
**Note**
If the subjects linked by "and" are used as one phrase, or constitute one idea, then the verb must be singular

The color of his socks and shoe is black.
Here "socks and shoe" are two nouns, however the subject is "color" which is singular.

# PRACTICE TEST QUESTIONS SET 1

The questions below are not the same as you will find on the Corrections Officer - that would be too easy! And nobody knows what the questions will be and they change all the time. Below are general questions that cover the same subject areas as the Corrections Officer. So, while the format and exact wording of the questions may differ slightly, and change from year to year, if you can answer the questions below, you will have no problem with the Corrections Officer exam.

For the best results, take these Practice Test Questions as if it were the real exam. Set aside time when you will not be disturbed, and a location that is quiet and free of distractions. Read the instructions carefully, read each question carefully, and answer to the best of your ability.
Use the bubble answer sheets provided.

Do not attempt more than one set of practice test questions in one day. After completing the first practice test, wait two or three days before attempting the second set of questions.

# SITUATIONAL JUDGEMENT

|     | A | B | C | D | E |     | A | B | C | D | E |
|-----|---|---|---|---|---|-----|---|---|---|---|---|
| 1   | ○ | ○ | ○ | ○ | ○ | 26  | ○ | ○ | ○ | ○ | ○ |
| 2   | ○ | ○ | ○ | ○ | ○ | 27  | ○ | ○ | ○ | ○ | ○ |
| 3   | ○ | ○ | ○ | ○ | ○ | 28  | ○ | ○ | ○ | ○ | ○ |
| 4   | ○ | ○ | ○ | ○ | ○ | 29  | ○ | ○ | ○ | ○ | ○ |
| 5   | ○ | ○ | ○ | ○ | ○ | 30  | ○ | ○ | ○ | ○ | ○ |
| 6   | ○ | ○ | ○ | ○ | ○ | 31  | ○ | ○ | ○ | ○ | ○ |
| 7   | ○ | ○ | ○ | ○ | ○ | 32  | ○ | ○ | ○ | ○ | ○ |
| 8   | ○ | ○ | ○ | ○ | ○ | 33  | ○ | ○ | ○ | ○ | ○ |
| 9   | ○ | ○ | ○ | ○ | ○ | 34  | ○ | ○ | ○ | ○ | ○ |
| 10  | ○ | ○ | ○ | ○ | ○ | 35  | ○ | ○ | ○ | ○ | ○ |
| 11  | ○ | ○ | ○ | ○ | ○ | 36  | ○ | ○ | ○ | ○ | ○ |
| 12  | ○ | ○ | ○ | ○ | ○ | 37  | ○ | ○ | ○ | ○ | ○ |
| 13  | ○ | ○ | ○ | ○ | ○ | 38  | ○ | ○ | ○ | ○ | ○ |
| 14  | ○ | ○ | ○ | ○ | ○ | 39  | ○ | ○ | ○ | ○ | ○ |
| 15  | ○ | ○ | ○ | ○ | ○ | 40  | ○ | ○ | ○ | ○ | ○ |
| 16  | ○ | ○ | ○ | ○ | ○ |     |   |   |   |   |   |
| 17  | ○ | ○ | ○ | ○ | ○ |     |   |   |   |   |   |
| 18  | ○ | ○ | ○ | ○ | ○ |     |   |   |   |   |   |
| 19  | ○ | ○ | ○ | ○ | ○ |     |   |   |   |   |   |
| 20  | ○ | ○ | ○ | ○ | ○ |     |   |   |   |   |   |
| 21  | ○ | ○ | ○ | ○ | ○ |     |   |   |   |   |   |
| 22  | ○ | ○ | ○ | ○ | ○ |     |   |   |   |   |   |
| 23  | ○ | ○ | ○ | ○ | ○ |     |   |   |   |   |   |
| 24  | ○ | ○ | ○ | ○ | ○ |     |   |   |   |   |   |
| 25  | ○ | ○ | ○ | ○ | ○ |     |   |   |   |   |   |

## SENTENCE ORDER

1. __ __ __ __ __ __

2. __ __ __ __ __ __

3. __ __ __ __ __ __

4. __ __ __ __ __ __

5. __ __ __ __ __ __

# READING AND SENTENCE CORRECTION

|    | A | B | C | D |
|----|---|---|---|---|
| 1  | ○ | ○ | ○ | ○ |
| 2  | ○ | ○ | ○ | ○ |
| 3  | ○ | ○ | ○ | ○ |
| 4  | ○ | ○ | ○ | ○ |
| 5  | ○ | ○ | ○ | ○ |
| 6  | ○ | ○ | ○ | ○ |
| 7  | ○ | ○ | ○ | ○ |
| 8  | ○ | ○ | ○ | ○ |
| 9  | ○ | ○ | ○ | ○ |
| 10 | ○ | ○ | ○ | ○ |
| 11 | ○ | ○ | ○ | ○ |
| 12 | ○ | ○ | ○ | ○ |
| 13 | ○ | ○ | ○ | ○ |
| 14 | ○ | ○ | ○ | ○ |
| 15 | ○ | ○ | ○ | ○ |
| 16 | ○ | ○ | ○ | ○ |
| 17 | ○ | ○ | ○ | ○ |
| 18 | ○ | ○ | ○ | ○ |
| 19 | ○ | ○ | ○ | ○ |
| 20 | ○ | ○ | ○ | ○ |

# VOCABULARY

|    | A | B | C | D |
|----|---|---|---|---|
| 1  | ○ | ○ | ○ | ○ |
| 2  | ○ | ○ | ○ | ○ |
| 3  | ○ | ○ | ○ | ○ |
| 4  | ○ | ○ | ○ | ○ |
| 5  | ○ | ○ | ○ | ○ |
| 6  | ○ | ○ | ○ | ○ |
| 7  | ○ | ○ | ○ | ○ |
| 8  | ○ | ○ | ○ | ○ |
| 9  | ○ | ○ | ○ | ○ |
| 10 | ○ | ○ | ○ | ○ |
| 11 | ○ | ○ | ○ | ○ |
| 12 | ○ | ○ | ○ | ○ |
| 13 | ○ | ○ | ○ | ○ |
| 14 | ○ | ○ | ○ | ○ |
| 15 | ○ | ○ | ○ | ○ |
| 16 | ○ | ○ | ○ | ○ |
| 17 | ○ | ○ | ○ | ○ |
| 18 | ○ | ○ | ○ | ○ |
| 19 | ○ | ○ | ○ | ○ |
| 20 | ○ | ○ | ○ | ○ |

# ENGLISH GRAMMAR

|     | A | B | C | D | E |     | A | B | C | D | E |
| --- | - | - | - | - | - | --- | - | - | - | - | - |
| 1   | ○ | ○ | ○ | ○ | ○ | 21  | ○ | ○ | ○ | ○ | ○ |
| 2   | ○ | ○ | ○ | ○ | ○ | 22  | ○ | ○ | ○ | ○ | ○ |
| 3   | ○ | ○ | ○ | ○ | ○ | 23  | ○ | ○ | ○ | ○ | ○ |
| 4   | ○ | ○ | ○ | ○ | ○ | 24  | ○ | ○ | ○ | ○ | ○ |
| 5   | ○ | ○ | ○ | ○ | ○ | 25  | ○ | ○ | ○ | ○ | ○ |
| 6   | ○ | ○ | ○ | ○ | ○ | 26  | ○ | ○ | ○ | ○ | ○ |
| 7   | ○ | ○ | ○ | ○ | ○ | 27  | ○ | ○ | ○ | ○ | ○ |
| 8   | ○ | ○ | ○ | ○ | ○ | 28  | ○ | ○ | ○ | ○ | ○ |
| 9   | ○ | ○ | ○ | ○ | ○ | 29  | ○ | ○ | ○ | ○ | ○ |
| 10  | ○ | ○ | ○ | ○ | ○ | 30  | ○ | ○ | ○ | ○ | ○ |
| 11  | ○ | ○ | ○ | ○ | ○ | 31  | ○ | ○ | ○ | ○ | ○ |
| 12  | ○ | ○ | ○ | ○ | ○ | 32  | ○ | ○ | ○ | ○ | ○ |
| 13  | ○ | ○ | ○ | ○ | ○ | 33  | ○ | ○ | ○ | ○ | ○ |
| 14  | ○ | ○ | ○ | ○ | ○ | 34  | ○ | ○ | ○ | ○ | ○ |
| 15  | ○ | ○ | ○ | ○ | ○ | 35  | ○ | ○ | ○ | ○ | ○ |
| 16  | ○ | ○ | ○ | ○ | ○ | 36  | ○ | ○ | ○ | ○ | ○ |
| 17  | ○ | ○ | ○ | ○ | ○ | 37  | ○ | ○ | ○ | ○ | ○ |
| 18  | ○ | ○ | ○ | ○ | ○ | 38  | ○ | ○ | ○ | ○ | ○ |
| 19  | ○ | ○ | ○ | ○ | ○ | 39  | ○ | ○ | ○ | ○ | ○ |
| 20  | ○ | ○ | ○ | ○ | ○ | 40  | ○ | ○ | ○ | ○ | ○ |

# SITUATIONAL JUDGEMENT

## 1. Scenario

You have assigned your team some work with a tight deadline which unless met means that the company is going to incur huge losses. You assign Jackie is to lead the team delivering the assignment. Two days before the deadline, Jackie shows up in your office and explains to you that it will not be possible to deliver the project on time because one of the team members failed to play his part. How are you going to handle the situation?

    a. Quarrel with Jackie and blame the delay on her entirely as a team leader.

    b. Brainstorm with her on what may be done to cover up the undone work.

    c. Ensure that both Jackie and the employee get a salary cut.

    d. Call a meeting and shame the entire team for failing.

## 2. Scenario

A customer calls in with a list of complaints about your company. The sales representative directs the client to your office. The customer is angry and dissatisfied with their purchases. How do you communicate with the dissatisfied customer?

    a. Explain to the customer why they are wrong and how right your argument is.

    b. Listen carefully to the complaint without interrupting, show empathy and understanding and offer the best assistance you can.

    c. Blame the customer for not reading the terms and conditions of purchase

    d. Deny a refund and refer the customer to another company.

## 3. Scenario

A lot of shipments have been directed to your department which is currently short-staffed. The supervisor asks all employees to take turns working  overtime to handle the situation. You feel worn-out having worked late more than once during the week. You and your friends have plans to go out on Friday evening but your supervisor asks you to cover for a sick colleague. How would you respond?

    a. Explain to the supervisor that those plans are hard to change because you waited two summers to re-unite with your college friends.

    b. Accept the work and turn your friends down.

    c. Ignore the order and go out anyway.

    d. Communicate with your team members and supervisor and see if there is another solution, and if not you may have to miss your planned outing.

## 4. Scenario

You have been working with a company for more than three years. During this period, you have familiarized yourself with all polices governing the company's operations. On this particular day, your immediate supervisor asks you to undertake a task which definitely goes against company policies. What should you do?

    a. Do as the supervisor asks and disregard the company policies

    b. Decline to do what the supervisor asks of you.

    c. Explain to the supervisor that the action goes against he policies

    d. Ask the supervisor whether he knows the policies of the company

## 5. Scenario

You are working on a task that calls for abilities that you don't have. You need help from your work mates who possess the required skills. How would you go about seeking collaboration with these employees?

a. Make a thorough analysis of all the parameters at play and act decisively.

b. Ask for collaboration from other team members on the appropriate course of action.

c. Act immediately without thinking

d. Fail to take any action

## 6. Scenario

One of the projects assigned to you involves a client, Jane. She keeps calling you to make changes to the original plan. It is your feeling now that Jane is changing most of the projects specifics which could directly impact the budget. How would you deal with this situation?

a. Propose that she makes all changes in an official manner, through letters and email.

b. Take her orders and do as she pleases to ensure customer satisfaction.

c. Refuse to do what she asks outside the initial contract or agreement.

d. Discuss this with your superiors and find a way forward.

## 7. Scenario

A client is very much opposed to your point of view. It is important that they are convinced of your idea. How would you go about making the client see things from your perspective?

a. Begin with understanding and seeing things in your client's perspective.

b. Begin with explaining your point of view to the client in clear and simple terms.

c. Decode what your client could be thinking about

d. Sit the client down and prove to him why he is wrong

## 8. Scenario

Conflict in the workplace is common in most organizations. Your co-worker falsely accuses you and you feel resentment towards him. The two of you get into an extended conflict and antagonistic relationship, which could see production effected. How should you handle this situation?

a. Apologize to your coworker.

b. Have a supervisor involved in resolving the conflict.

c. Act normal and pretend that nothing wrong will happen.

d. Ask for an apology from your friend.

## 9. Scenario

You are on shift and performing your normal duties, when something very urgent comes up. The issue is extremely demanding and none of your colleagues have handled this type of situation before. How should you handle this situation?

a. Make a thorough analysis of all the parameters at play and act decisively.

b. Ask for collaboration from other team members on the appropriate course of action.

c. Act immediately without thinking

d. Fail to take any action

## 10. Scenario

It's one bright Monday morning and you show up to work as usual. Before you get to the main door, you over-hear your coworkers shouting and yelling at each other. It seems like a really big fight is going on. It's obvious that your coworkers disagree on some very basic principles. How should you go about bringing cohesion in such a team?

    a. Refer this matter to your supervisor

    b. Ask what could be wrong and offer advice

    c. Talk to each of the employees separately

    d. Discuss this with the entire team and ask for solutions

## 11. Scenario

An editor complains about your work regardless of how much you try. How should you deal with a difficult supervisor?

    a. Ignore his negative comments and stay positive

    b. Listen attentively to the feedback and try to follow.

    c. Refer to the company's policy document for further information.

    d. Blame the supervisor for being ignorant.

## 12. Scenario

Workload is increasingly becoming a problem in your department. How should you work to improve the situation?

    a. Assign more work to a junior employees

    b. Request more staff or temporary help from the management

    c. Ask for higher pay for you and your team

    d. Do what you can and leave what you can't

### 13. Scenario

Your team goes out for a party but there is a line-up and the wait time is too long.  Some of your team grow impatient and want to leave.  How should you handle this situation?

    a. Offer incentives and ask them to be patient

    b. Request them to be patient for a little while longer

    c. Lead them in demonstrating against the unfair treatment

    d. Keep quiet and let things fall into place

### 14. Scenario

Suppose you fail while undertaking a project given to you by your supervisor. How should you react?

    a. Freak out and blame the failure on yourself and your team

    b.  Ensure that you learn from the mistakes and move on to become a better employee

    c.  Ignore the failure and console yourself that failure is inevitable

    d.  None of the above

### 15. Scenario

You have been given an assignment together with a colleague.  When you need crucial information, your colleague takes too long time to respond. What should you do?

    a. Discuss with your colleague and see if there is a solution.

    b. Discuss the matter with your immediate supervisor.

    c. Demand that he keeps you posted at all times and respond faster.

    d. Acquire information from other sources on your own.

## 16. Scenario

The company you work for goes undergoes various changes. You, and some of the employees are finding it hard to adjust to rapid and constant changes. How should you act in such a situation?

 a. Rebel against the proposed changes.

 b. Read new company books to improve yourself.

 c. Mobilize other employees to attend training.

 d. Become more actively involved in the changes.

## 17. Scenario

As a team leader, your company assigns you with a huge project. How should you go about achieving the goals set by the company?

 a. Explain the project and goals to everyone.

 b. Involve only the people you deem important to avoid confusion.

 c. Ask for assistance from the experienced supervisors.

 d. Decline any assistance from anybody who may deter your project.

## 18. Scenario

You are in charge of a team that looks up to you for many things not just on work related issues. You learn some very bad news which needs to be delivered to your team. How do you go about it?

 a. Be straight forward and direct.

 b. Avoid addressing issues that could be unwelcome to the team.

 c. Bring them together and explain but insure others outside the team are to blame.

 d. Ask someone else to deliver the bad news on your behalf.

**19. Scenario**

You notice that your team members are actively competing against each other on a project you are overseeing. How should you react?

a. Discourage any sort of competition.

b. Monitor the competition to ensure that it's healthy and productive towards achieving the goals.

c. Allow unregulated competition where the smartest wins.

d. Offer a reward for the most productive.

**20. Scenario**

You face a lot of criticism at work for something you did. This weighs you down and affects your general performance.

What should you do?

a. Find areas to criticize those criticizing you.

b. Let the matter be addressed by your supervisors.

c. Resent the critic.

d. Work on improving the aspect criticized by my colleagues.

**21. Scenario**

After working on a project for several months, it comes clear that reorganizing the team is inevitable to complete the project. What should you do?

a. Discard the current team and form another.

b. Match the strengths of the team members with the overall goals stipulated.

c. Remove the less skilled employees and replace them with more experienced ones.

d. Do nothing.

## 22. Scenario

Some of the junior employees in your company are not under your jurisdiction yet their co-operation is important for the success of your business. How should you save the situation?

    a. Demand for cooperation from them.

    b. Call them to a meeting and stress on the fact that you are a boss and they need to cooperate.

    c. Clearly communicate your ideas and be open to feedback.

    d. Request their supervisors to order them to cooperate with your department.

## 23. Scenario

You are the manger of a department. John, a junior employee, disregards orders given by you. How should you handle such a situation?

    a. Request that the employee is fired immediately.

    b. Set an example by disciplining the rogue employee.

    c. Hear out and understand the reason for his disagreement.

    d. Change the directive.

## 24. Scenario

New facts come to your attention mid-way through a project. They require you to change most or all of your plan. How do you go about changing the decisions already made?

    a.  Always keep clear communication between and among the members of the team.

    b.  Abruptly change the initial plan.

    c.  Consult with others on what needs to be done.

    d.  Disregard the new facts.

## 25. Scenario

One of your employees disagrees with you purely on matters concerning business. How do you go about formulating and presenting your argument without hurting them?

    a. Rebuke the employee for disobedience.

    b. Over-rule the objections.

    c. Base your argument on objective facts and listen to their side of the argument.

    d. Call for disciplinary action against the employee.

## 26. Scenario

An agent has worked tirelessly with a client with no success. This client is then referred to you for assistance. How should you go about assisting the client?

    a.  Refer the client to another agent who is more competent.

    b.  Refuse to accept the client.

    c.  Listen attentively to the issue troubling the client and offer professional assistance as you deem best.

    d.  Attend to the client similar to how he has been attended in the past.

## 27. Scenario

The company you are working for has in the past experienced communication hiccups and misunderstandings. How should you prevent similar incidents in the future?

    a.  Encourage all employees to use written communication.

    b.  Make clarifications where needed and encourage team members to do the same.

    c.  Refuse to consider any verbal communication.

    d.  Be complacent in communicating with others.

### 28. Scenario

A workmate is very mean to you. You disregard this but the issue has recently been putting a lot pressure on you. You need to stay positive and motivated. How should you handle this?

    a. Be mean to them as well.

    b. Confront his ill behavior.

    c. Involve supervisors in resolving the conflict.

    d. Keep on motivating yourself to become better.

### 29. Scenario

A client walks into your office requesting assistance with product knowledge. Since you are less involved in this area and cannot help him. How should you handle the situation?

    a. Refer the client to the correct department.

    b. Welcome the client and be as hospitable as possible as you find the right person to assist him.

    c. Find the correct information and assist the client.

    d. Inform the client that the areas requested is outside your scope.

### 30. Scenario

A client you have been serving becomes impatience with the process. She goes out looking for the manager saying that you are taking too long to give her the assistance she is requesting. What should you do to diffuse the situation?

    a. Refuse to attend the client.

    b. Take this matter to your supervisor.

    c. Explain the process to the client why it is taking longer.

    d. Ignore the client completely.

## 31. Scenario

Daniel is working on a project that seems to give him a lot of problems. He has shown signs of depression in the last week. What should you do to help him out?

a.  Motivate Daniel.

b.  Inform the supervisors.

c.  Take him for some counseling sessions.

d.  Do absolutely nothing.

## 32. Scenario

A sales seminar you attend insists that to close more sales, you need to work on making a better first impression. What should you do to close more sales?

a.  Dress smartly and speak clearly.

b.  Conduct business as usual.

c.  Dramatize your ideas to create rapport.

d.  Ignore the advice from the supervisor.

## 33. Scenario

You are required to collaborate with a coworker who has proven tough to please. But for the success of the project, both of you need to work together. How should you go about such a scenario?

a  Request their partnership.

b.  Buy some good stuff to please your coworker.

c.  Involve your manager to bring in some understanding.

d.  Discuss on the issues between you and agree to work together.

## 34. Scenario

As an employee of many years in a certain company, you feel totally demotivated and dissatisfied with your work. You need to improve. What are you likely to do to achieve your objectives?

    a.  Find a new place to work.

    b.  Find new tasks to re-engage your interest.

    c.  Listen to motivational speeches.

    d.  Learn to always stay positive.

## 35. Scenario

Some of your team members are less committed than in the recent past. How should you go about improving commitment?

    a.  Introduce work incentives.

    b.  Reduce compensation for the employees who are not producing.

    c.  Talk to the employees on the need of being committed.

    d.  Fire the team and get another team.

## 36. Scenario

Sam, a 30 year-old employee in your organization has shown exemplary work. You want to praise his work in front of the other employees. How should you go about praising him?

    a.  Wait until everyone is together and compliment him.

    b.  Contrast his work with the poor work of the others.

    c.  Email all the employees.

    d.  Ignore this idea.

### 37. Scenario

While working with your team members on a project you realize that things are not going well. How should you motivate the team to perform better?

   a. Meet regularly to discuss on issues.

   b. Explain how lucky they are.

   c. Select the best team players and assign them more responsibility.

   d. Become actively involved in daily operations of the business.

### 38. Scenario

Most of the strategies you have adopted thus far don't seem to be working in getting team to do the right thing. You feel the need to set an example. How should you go about this?

   a. Work twice as hard.

   b. Report to work early and leave late.

   c. Lecture the team to strive to be like you.

   d. Condemn the team for being lazy.

### 39. Scenario

You have formulated the goals of your department along with your team members. However, you realize that you are not yet sure on how those goals are going to be achieved. How should you go about such a situation?

   a. Read and re-read the goals for full comprehension.

   b. Ensure team members understand what is required of them.

   c. Brainstorm on ideas that could get you to your goal.

   d. Just do the work anyhow.

### 40. Scenario

You are in a fast-paced environment and your job demands that you achieve the set objectives. This, according to you is a real challenge. How should you achieve your objectives?

a. Let the team know the deadlines to the set objectives.

b. Keep the information to yourself.

c. Work three times harder.

d. Use the internet to learn more.

## SENTENCE ORDER

**Instructions:** The first sentence of a paragraph is given below, followed by additional sentences in the paragraph, listed in no particular order.  Order the sentences to create the best paragraph.  Make sure the paragraph is properly organized and grammatically correct.

**1. Making a movie is an overwhelmingly scary creative process.**

A. All of those people specialize in carrying out one small portion of the creative process of movie making.

B. Those ideas need to be executed by more than just the director and producer.

C. Without a team of over 200 people, most major motion pictures could not be successfully completed.

D. With so many people involved in making a movie, there are bound to be overwhelming challenges that can stump and frighten even the best producers and directors.

E. The reason they are so scary is because they are made up of thousands of individual ideas about setting, characters, lighting, and storytelling.

**2. Crocodiles are becoming more difficult to find in Jamaica.**

A. Even though hunting crocodiles is illegal, there is so little money in Jamaica so no one is being punished by government agencies.

B. For decades, crocodiles graced the Jamaican Coat of Arms as well as decorated military vehicles because they have been such a common sight along the beaches and salty waterways.

C. Since the people of Jamaica fear the large reptiles, they have also looked the other way in regards to the increase in crocodile poaching, too.

D. The biggest reason that crocodiles are disappearing is because they are a tasty delicacy and their meat can bring about $35 per pound.

E. Now, conservationists are worried that crocodiles might disappear completely from the tropical paradise.

**3. If you are looking to start a small business or raise money for an important cause, crowd-funding is a great tool to help raise money.**

A. One of first uses of crowd-funding happened in 1884, when Joseph Pulitzer asked Americans to send money to help build the base of the Statue of Liberty; many people donated less than $1, but over $100,000 was raised.

B. There are currently over 400 online platforms that project creators can use to try to raise money.

C. Today, crowd-funding is carried out on the Internet.

D. The project creators use those platforms to build profiles about their organizations to market their ideas while engaging audiences to entice them to give their money to help get the ideas off of the ground.

E. He used his newspaper to ask people to donate.

**4. In the politically isolated North Korea, the most popular snack food is one that originated in Tennessee in the 1920s: the Choco Pie.**

A. This company has a foothold in South Korea and many of the South Korean Choco Pies have made their way into North Korea through black market routes.

B. Today, the pies are so popular in North Korea that they are used in lieu of cash, since cash is not allowed in the communist country.

C. The Choco Pie made its way to Asian nations during World War II and the Korean War.

D. In the 2000s, the Choco Pie was made by a company called Orion.

E. This little treat is similar to the Moon Pie, which is a graham cracker sandwich filled with marshmallow and covered in tasty chocolate.

**5. Fracking is a current controversial issue, but many people have no idea what it actually is.**

A. The first well is dug so that geologists can learn about the rocks in that area.

B. The second step involves horizontal drilling, which is called fracking.

C. Fracking is actually a process with three necessary steps.

D. Finally, the fracking allows energy companies to collect the gas that is released by the horizontal drilling.

E. The first step includes building a vertical well.

**Directions:** The following questions are based on several reading passages. A series of questions follow each passage. Read each passage carefully, and then answer the questions based on it. You may reread the passage as often as you wish. When you have finished answering the questions based on one passage, go right onto the next passage. Choose the best answer based on the information given and implied.

## READING

**Questions 1 refers to the following passage.**

### The Life of Helen Keller

Many people have heard of Helen Keller. She is famous because she was unable to see or hear, but learned to speak and read and went onto attend college and earn a degree. Her life is a very interesting story, one that she developed into an autobiography, which was then adapted into both a stage play and a movie. How did Helen Keller overcome her disabilities to become a famous woman? Read on to find out. Helen Keller was not born blind and deaf. When she was a small baby, she had a very high fever for several days. As a result of her sudden illness, baby Helen lost her eyesight and her hearing. Because she was so young when she went deaf and blind, Helen Keller never had any recollection of being able to see or hear. Since she could not hear, she could not learn to talk. Since she could not see, it was difficult for her to move around. For the first six years of her life, her world was very still and dark.

Imagine what Helen's childhood was like. She could not hear her mother's voice. She could not see the beauty of her parent's farm. She could not recognize who was giving her a hug, or a bath or even where her bedroom was each night. Worse, she could not communicate with her parents in any way. She could not express her feelings or tell them the things she wanted. It must have been a very sad childhood.

When Helen was six years old, her parents hired her a teacher named Anne Sullivan. Anne was a young woman who was almost blind. However, she could hear and she could read Braille, so she was a perfect teacher for young Helen.  At first, Anne had a very hard time teaching Helen anything. She described her first impression of Helen as a "wild thing, not a child."  Helen did not like Anne at first either. She bit and hit Anne when Anne tried to teach her. However, the two of them eventually came to have a great deal of love and respect.

Anne taught Helen to hear by putting her hands on people's throats. She could feel the sounds people made. In time, Helen learned to feel what people said.  Next, Anne taught Helen to read Braille, which is a way that books are written for the blind. Finally, Anne taught Helen to talk. Although Helen did learn to talk, it was hard for anyone but Anne to understand her.

As Helen grew older, she amazed more and more people with her story. She went to college and wrote books about her life. She gave talks to the public, with Anne at her side, translating her words. Today, both Anne Sullivan and Helen Keller are famous women who are respected for their lives' work.

**1. Helen Keller learned to speak but Anne translated her words when she spoke in public. The reason Helen needed a translator was because**

    a. Helen spoke another language.

    b. Helen's words were hard for people to understand.

    c. Helen spoke very quietly.

    d. Helen did not speak but only used sign language.

**Questions 2 refers to the following passage.**

## Ways Characters Communicate in Theatre

Playwrights give their characters voices in a way that gives depth and added meaning to what happens on stage during their play. There are different types of speech in scripts that allow characters to talk with themselves, with other characters, and even with the audience.

It is very unique to theatre that characters may talk "to themselves." When characters do this, the speech they give is called a soliloquy. Soliloquies are usually poetic, introspective, moving, and can tell audience members about the feelings, motivations, or suspicions of an individual character without that character having to reveal them to other characters on stage. "To be or not to be" is a famous soliloquy given by Hamlet as he considers difficult but important themes, such as life and death.

The most common type of communication in plays is when one character is speaking to another or a group of other characters. This is generally called dialogue, but can also be called monologue if one character speaks without being interrupted for a long time. It is not necessarily the most important type of communication, but it is the most common because the plot of the play cannot really progress without it.

Lastly, and most unique to theatre (although it has been used somewhat in film) is when a character speaks directly to the audience. This is called an aside, and scripts usually specifically direct actors to do this. Asides are usually comical, an inside joke between the character and the audience, and very short. The actor will usually face the audience when delivering them, even if it's for a moment, so the audience can recognize this move as an aside.

All three of these types of communication are important to the art of theatre, and have been perfected by famous playwrights like Shakespeare. Understanding these types of communication can help an audience member grasp what is artful about the script and action of a play.

**2. According to the passage, characters in plays communicate to**

a. move the plot forward

b. show the private thoughts and feelings of one character

c. make the audience laugh

d. add beauty and artistry to the play

**Questions 3 - 6 refer to the following passage.**

**When a Poet Longs to Mourn, He Writes an Elegy**

Poems are an expressive, especially emotional, form of writing. They have been present in literature virtually from the time civilizations invented the written word. Poets often portrayed as moody, secluded, and even troubled, but this is because poets are introspective and feel deeply about the current events and cultural norms they are surrounded with. Poets often produce the most telling literature, giving insight into the society and mind-set they come from. This can be done in many forms.

The oldest types of poems often include many stanzas, may or may not rhyme, and are more about telling a story than experimenting with language or words. The most common types of ancient poetry are epics, which are usually extremely long stories that follow a hero through his journey, or ellegies, which are often solemn in tone and used to mourn or lament something or someone. The Mesopotamians are often said to have invented the written word, and their literature is among the oldest in the world, including the epic poem titled "Epic of Gilgamesh." Similar in style and length to "Gilgamesh" is "Beowulf," an ellegy written in Old English and set in Scandinavia. These poems are often used by professors as the earliest examples of literature.

The importance of poetry was revived in the Renaissance. At this time, Europeans discovered the style and beauty of ancient Greek arts, and poetry was among those. Shakespeare is the most well-known poet of the time, and he used poetry not only to write poems but also to write plays for the theatre. The most popular forms of poetry during the Renaissance included villanelles, (a nineteen-line poetic form) sonnets, as well as the epic. Poets during this time focused on style and form, and developed very specific rules and outlines for how an exceptional poem should be written.

As often happens in the arts, modern poets have rejected the constricting rules of Renaissance poets, and free form poems are much more popular. Some modern poems would read just like stories if they weren't arranged into lines and stanzas. It is difficult to tell which poems and poets will be the most important, because works of art often become more famous in hindsight, after the poet has died and society can look at itself without being in the moment. Modern poetry continues to develop, and will no doubt continue to change as values, thought, and writing continue to change.

Poems can be among the most enlightening and uplifting texts for a person to read if they are looking to connect with the past, connect with other people, or try to gain an understanding of what is happening in their time.

**3. In summary, the author has written this passage**

    a. as a foreword that will introduce a poem in a book or magazine

    b. because she loves poetry and wants more people to like it

    c. to give a brief history of poems

    d. to convince students to write poems

## 4. The author organizes the paragraphs mainly by

a. moving chronologically, explaining which types of poetry were common in that time

b. talking about new types of poems each paragraph and explaining them a little

c. focusing on one poet or group of people and the poems they wrote

d. explaining older types of poetry so she can talk about modern poetry

## 5. The author's claim that poetry has been around "virtually from the time civilizations invented the written word" is supported by the detail that

a. Beowulf is written in Old English, which is not really in use any longer

b. epic poems told stories about heroes

c. the Renaissance poets tried to copy Greek poets

d. the Mesopotamians are credited with both inventing the word and writing "Epic of Gilgamesh"

## 6. According to the passage, the word that the word "telling" means

a. speaking

b. significant

c. soothing

d. wordy

# CORRECTING SENTENCES

## Questions 7 - 10 refer to the following passage

Mankind's thirst for knowledge about ourselves and the universe has always been insatiable, making curiosity a driving force for human advances through history. [1] Not only that, human curiosity and creativity have created countless works of fiction that speculate about future discoveries. [2]

Our neighboring planet Mars, for example, has long led scientists and writers to generate stories about living on the Red Planet. [3] Serious endeavors in science and technology are motivated by our never-ending questions. [4] So far, NASA has carried out several exploratory missions to Mars and the rover robot Curiosity is the latest and most sophisticated. [5]

Curiosity was launched in late November 2011 from Cape Canaveral Air Force Station in Florida. [6] It successfully landed on Mars on August 6, 2012 searching for evidence of life. [7] The car sized robot, weighing about a ton, is equipped with all the technical capacities to carry out its mission to explore our neighbor for biological, geological and geochemical traces of life. [8] It will also test the Martian soil and surface to collect data about its planetary evolution and surface radiation. [9]

Curiosity has been engineered with cutting-edge technologies worth over 2.5 billion US dollars. [10] The most incredible component of the rover is the on-board science lab. [11] Apart from that, it consists of a communications system that allows transmission of commands to the rover from the control centre at NASA, enabling direct control of the robot's activities on the surface of the Red Planet. [12] The Curiosity rover has a number of mounted cameras which assists navigation, as well as capturing images from the Martian surface and transmitting them back to Earth. [13]

**7. How would you re-write sentence 1?**

a. No changes

b. Mankind's thirst for knowledge has always been insatiable, making curiosity a driving factor for human advances through history.

c. Mankind's thirst for knowledge is insatiable, making curiosity a driving factor for human advances through history.

d. Humankind's thirst for knowledge is insatiable, making curiosity a driving force in advances throughout history.

**8. Which sentence in the third paragraph is least relevant to the main idea of the third paragraph?**

a. 6

b. 8

c. 9

d. 10

**9. Which of the following changes would focus attention on the main idea of the last paragraph?**

a. To achieve its goals, Curiosity has been engineered with cutting-edge technologies worth over 2.5 billion US dollars.

b. Because a lot of funding was available for this project, Curiosity has been engineered with cutting-edge technologies worth over 2.5 billion US dollars.

c. As there is no guarantee that it will succeed in its mission, Curiosity has been engineered with cutting-edge technologies worth over 2.5 billion US dollars.

d. NASA's scientific data is so reliable that, being assured of no risk of failure in the mission, Curiosity has been engineered with cutting-edge technologies worth over 2.5 billion US dollars.

## 10. Which of the following is/are needed in sentence 5?

a. So far, "NASA" has carried out several exploration missions to Mars and the rover robot Curiosity is the latest and most sophisticated of all.

b. So far, NASA has carried out several exploratory missions to Mars and the rover robot Curiosity is the latest and most sophisticated of all.

c. So far, NASA has carried out several exploration missions to Mars and the rover robot -Curiosity- is the latest and most sophisticated of all.

d. So far, NASA has carried out several exploratory missions to Mars and the rover robot "Curiosity" is the latest and most sophisticated of all.

## Green Energy from Olive Oil

**Questions 11 - 14 refer to the following passage**

The debate over developing sustainable energy sources have been very active in the past two decades. [1] With continued concern over global climate change, environmentalists are urging governments for lowering their dependence on fossil fuels in order for ensuring reduced carbon emission into the atmosphere. [2] Consequently, governments worldwide are turning their attention to the search for non-emissive sources of energy. [3] Renewable substitutes under extensive research are solar power, wind, geothermal energy and harnessing energy from ocean waves. [4]

While the search for environment friendly energy sources is already under way, developing these alternatives at a reasonable cost is a major challenge. [5] No cost-effective replacement for fossil fuels has yet been found. [6] However, recent years have seen remarkable progress in the field of solar energy. [7] Ted Sargent, a Professor at University of Toronto, Canada, has discovered that olive oil has the capacity to capture solar radiation and emit electrons resulting in an electric current. [8] This is a major discovery in the solar power generation industry as it offers a cheap source of harnessing the Sun's energy. [9]

Oleic acid, the main ingredient of olive oil, absorbs infrared radiation is the major component of the Sun's radiation reaching the Earth. [10] The discovery is significant because so far, no attempt has been made to use the abundant infrared radiation we receive throughout the year. [11] Capturing this heat wave radiation, along with the photons that are present in sunlight, increases the efficiency of the solar cells that are already being manufactured commercially. [12] And to make it possible, Professor Sargent has developed a new kind of solar cell called "quantum dots," tiny cells made from gels of tin, bismuth, lead, sulphur and selenium mixed with extra pure olive oil. [13] The resulting ink-like crystal absorbs both photons and infrared radiation and has the capacity to transmit electrons and produce a current. [14]

This new method of capturing the Sun's energy is considered a breakthrough in the solar power industry as it offers cheaper alternatives to the existing use of silicon crystals which are costly to manufacture. [15] And although the invention is yet to prove its efficiency, a lot of funding has already been dedicated to further research. [16]

**11. What sentence from the passage is an example of a sentence fragment?**

    a. 6

    b. 10

    c. 11

    d. 13

**12. Which of the following sentences should be deleted to reduce redundancy?**

    a. 5

    b. 6

    c. 9

    d. 15

**13. Which of the following changes are needed in sentence 10?**

a. Oleic acid, the main ingredient of olive oil, absorbs infrared radiation is the major component of the Sun's radiation reaching the Earth.

b. Oleic acid, the main ingredient of olive oil, absorbs infrared radiation, which is the major component of the Sun's radiation reaching the Earth.

c. Oleic acid, the main ingredient of olive oil absorbs infrared radiation that is the major component of the Sun's radiation reaching the Earth.

d. Oleic acid, the main ingredient of olive oil, absorbs infrared radiation what is the major component of the Sun's radiation reaching the Earth.

**14. Which of the following changes are needed in sentence 2?**

a. With continued concern over global climate change, environmentalists are urging governments to lowering their dependence on fossil fuels to ensuring reduced carbon emission into the atmosphere.

b. With continued concern over global climate change, environmentalists are urging governments lower their dependence on fossil fuels in order for ensuring reduced carbon emission into the atmosphere.

c. With continued concern over global climate change, environmentalists are urging governments to lower their dependence on fossil fuels in order for ensuring reduced carbon emission into the atmosphere.

d. With continued concern over global climate change, environmentalists are urging governments to lower their dependence on fossil fuels to ensure reduced carbon emission into the atmosphere.

# Hunting Lost Cities from Space

**Questions 15 - 18 refer to the following passage**

Satellite imaging has become widespread with improvements in telecommunication over the past two decades. [1] Communication satellites in orbit around the Earth have enabled large-scale mapping of the planet's surface which has become freely available thanks to technology giants like Google. [2] Satellite mapping has opened up new possibilities in diverse fields of science and technology. [3]

The key feature of the new tool, according to Professor Sarah Parcak, who discovered many cities, temples and pyramids covered under sands and sediment; is that it offers a wider perspective in size and scale of the location under study. [4] Along with the visual information that the satellite images provide, numerous details about the sites can be obtained from infrared (IR) and gravitational field images. [5] This information, coupled with conventional on-site procedures, are vital for archeology. [6]

IR data collected from satellite imaging provide clues about the activities of humans living in the contemporary times of their civilizations- including their agriculture, vegetation, structures, habitation roads and much more. [7] This type of information is derived from IR imagery which detects IR radiation present in sunlight as it is reflected by the Earth. [8] Different points in a civilization reflect IR radiation in different proportions, revealing the contrast between different areas and provide detailed insight about the causes of these differing heat signatures. [9]

**15. Which of the following changes in sentence 6 would focus attention on the main idea of the second paragraph?**

a. These information, along with a supply of some heavy machinery, will help the excavation of every archeological site accomplished within a short period of time.

b. This information, coupled with conventional on-site procedures, help archaeologists plan their excavation carefully and efficiently.

c. Such details are valuable records of ancient history and are essential assets of any civilization.

d. Such details, unfortunately, are available to archeological firms who are willing to invest a lot of money on putting satellites into orbit.

**16. Which of the following sentences should be modified to reduce redundancy?**

a. 7
b. 8
c. 9
d. 10

**17. Which of the following sentences, if inserted after sentence 3, would best illustrate the main idea of the passage?**

a. The application has inspired archaeologists to use it for searching for the traces of ancient civilizations and other anthropological dynamics.

b. The new technology will be very useful for excavation of archeological sites.

c. The application is a breakthrough for archeology and anthropology since it will allows us to zoom into the distant past to look for lost civilizations.

d. The concept has many positive aspects in the field of archeological science and excavation.

## 18. Which of the following change(s) is/are needed to sentence 4?

a. The key feature of the new tool- according to Professor Sarah Parcak, who discovered many cities, temples and pyramids covered under sands and sediment- is that it offers a wider perspective in size and scale of the location under study.

b. The key feature of the new tool- according to Professor Sarah Parcak- who discovered many cities, temples and pyramids covered under sands and sediment, is that it offers a wider perspective in size and scale of the location under study.

c. The key feature of the new tool according to Professor Sarah Parcak- who discovered many cities, temples and pyramids covered under sands and sediment- is that it offers a wider perspective in size and scale of the location under study.

d. The key feature of the new tool, according to Professor Sarah Parcak- who discovered many cities, temples and pyramids covered under sands and sediment is that it offers a wider perspective in size and scale of the location under study.

## Malala's Dream

**Questions 19 - 20 refer to the following passage**

Every child wants to attend school where they can interact, communicate with others and learn the art of life; discover themselves, socialize, have fun and make friends. [1] When they reach adolescence, children start framing their identity by making choices for their future career. [2] It was not so different with Malala Yousafzawi, who was an exemplary student and a responsible daughter since early childhood. [3] She always wanted to be a doctor, and upon entering her secondary school, started to work toward her dream. [4]

However, for girls in such a conservative society, where women's rights have little or no value, achieving such a lofty goal is pretty much impossible, not to mention the many other challenges of living in an unstable country like Pakistan. [5] Add to that an extreme conservative mentality that interferes in anyone's life whose world views do not match theirs. [6]

Malala's dreams were encountered with the obstacles that were also crushing the aspirations of millions of other young girls like her. [7] But unlike others who feared suppression and defamation, Malala stood up for her rights and looked to overcome the challenges facing her. [8] And while doing so, advanced the struggles of all girls like her with similar ambitions. [9] Persuaded by her father, who is a professional educator, she decided to give up her ambition of becoming a doctor and work for the education and establishment of girls in Mingora, a suburban town in Swat District. [10] In doing so, she had to sacrifice her own dreams, believing that at least millions other dreams will be fulfilled at the expense of just one. [1]1

Malala become a professional educator- campaigning for education for girls, side-by-side with her charismatic father who sponsored schools in the district where they live. [12] In the process, she somehow managed to uphold the courage to address the issues facing education for girls and proposed solutions for them. [13] Her sense of leadership soon made her popular among the local girls, and their parents, who supported her in fulfilling the educational rights of girls. [14] At the same time, however, Malala became the target of extremists. [15] She was shot in the head in an assassination attempt while she was returning home from school. [16]

**19. Which sentence is not consistent with the author's purpose?**

    a. 9

    b. 11

    c. 12

    d. 13

**20. Which of the following changes in sentence 10 would focus attention on the main idea of the second paragraph?**

a. Persuaded by her father, who is a professional educator, she sufficed in bearing a mediocre aim of becoming a simple schoolteacher and work for the education and establishment of girls in her locality, Mingora, a suburban town in Swat District.

b. Instructed by her father, who is a professional educator, she decided to give up her ambition of becoming a doctor and work for the education and establishment of girls in her locality, Mingora, a suburban town in Swat District.

c. Inspired by her father, who is a professional educator himself, she decided to work for the education and establishment of girls in her locality, Mingora, a suburban town in Swat District.

d. Contrary to her father, who is a professional educator, she persisted in becoming a doctor and vetoed to leave her father if he turned out to be an obstacle.

# VOCABULARY

**1. Choose a verb that means fearless or invulnerable to intimidation and fear.**

a. Feeble

b. Strongest

c. Dauntless

d. Super

**2. Choose a word that means the same as the underlined word.**

**I see the differences when they are placed side-by-side and <u>juxtaposed.</u>**

- a. Compared
- b. Eliminated
- c. Overturned
- d. Exonerated

**3. Choose the meaning of regicide.**

- a. v. To endow or furnish with requisite ability, character, knowledge and skill
- b. n. killing of a king
- c. adj. Disposed to seize by violence or by unlawful or greedy methods
- d. v. To refresh after labor

**4. Choose the best definition of pernicious.**

- a. Deadly
- b. Infectious
- c. Common
- d. Rare

**5. After she received her influenza vaccination, Nan thought that she was ________ to the common cold.**

- a. Immune
- b. Susceptible
- c. Vulnerable
- d. At risk

**6. She performed the gymnastics and stretches so well! I have never seen anyone so <u>nimble</u>.**

a. Awkward

b. Agile

c. Quick

d. Taut

**7. Are there any more <u>queries</u>?   We have already had so many questions today.**

a. Questions

b. Commands

c. Obfuscations

d. Paradoxes

**8. Choose a verb that means to remove a leader or high official from position.**

a. Sack

b. Suspend

c. Depose

d. Dropped

**9. Choose the best definition of pedestrian.**

a. Rare

b. Often

c. Walking or Running

d. Commonplace

**10.  Choose the best definition of petulant.**

a. Patient

b. Childish

c. Impatient

d. Mature

**11. Paul's rose bushes were being destroyed by Japanese beetles, so he invested in a good _______.**

    a. Fungicide

    b. Fertilizer

    c. Sprinkler

    d. Pesticide

**12. Choose the best definition of salient.**

    a. v. To make light by fermentation, as dough

    b. adj. Not stringent or energetic

    c. adj. negligible

    d. adj. worthy of note or relevant

**13. Choose the best definition of sedentary**

    a. n. A morbid condition, due to obstructed excretion of bile or characterized by yellowing of the skin

    b. adj. not moving or sitting at a place

    c. v. To wander from place to place

    d. n. Perplexity

**14. The last time that the crops failed, the entire nation experienced months of _______.**

    a. Famine

    b. Harvest

    c. Plenitude

    d. Disease

**15. Choose the best definition of stint.**

    a. Thrifty

    b. Annoyed

    c. Dislike

    d. Insult

**16. Choose the best definition of precipitate.**

a. To rain

b. To throw down

c. To throw up

d. to snow

**17. Choose the verb that means to build up or strengthen in relation to morals or religion.**

a. Sanctify

b. Amplify

c. Edify

d. Wry

**18. Choose the noun that means exit or way out.**

a. Door-jamb

b. Egress

c. Regress

d. Furtherance

**19. Choose the best definition of the underlined word.**

**The tide was in this morning but now it is starting to <u>recede</u>.**

a. Go out

b. Flow

c. Swell

d. Come in

**20. Choose the word that means private, personal.**

   a. Confidential

   b. Hysteric

   c. Simplistic

   d. Promissory

# ENGLISH GRAMMAR, PUNCTUATION, CAPITALIZATION AND USAGE

**Directions:** Carefully examine the underlined words in the sentences given below. You may see an error in punctuation, grammar, usage or capitalization. Select the correct version of the sentence from the choices given.

**1. To make chicken <u>soup; you</u> must first buy a chicken.**

   a. To make chicken soup you must first buy a chicken.

   b. To make chicken soup you must first, buy a chicken.

   c. To make chicken soup, you must first buy a chicken.

   d. None of the choices are correct.

**2. To travel around <u>the globe you have</u> to drive 25,000 miles.**

   a. To travel around the globe, you have to drive 25000 miles.

   b. To travel around the globe, you have to drive, 25000 miles.

   c. None of the choices are correct.

   d. To travel around the globe, you have to drive 25,000 miles.

**3. The dog loved chasing <u>bones; but never ate them:</u> it was running that he enjoyed.**

    a. The dog loved chasing bones, but never ate them; it was running that he enjoyed.

    b. The dog loved chasing bones; but never ate them, it was running that he enjoyed.

    c. The dog loved chasing bones, but never ate them, it was running that he enjoyed.

    d. None of the choices are correct.

**4. He had not paid the <u>rent, therefore,</u> the landlord changed the locks.**

    a. None of the choices are correct.

    b. He had not paid the rent; therefore, the landlord changed the locks.

    c. He had not paid the rent, therefore; the landlord changed the locks.

    d. He had not paid the rent therefore, the landlord changed the locks.

**5. If <u>he would have known</u> about the forecast, <u>he would have postponed</u> the camping trip.**

    a. He would have postponed the camping trip, if he would have known about the forecast.

    b. None of the choices are correct.

    c. If he have known about the forecast, he would have postponed the camping trip.

    d. If he had known about the forecast, he would have postponed the camping trip.

**6. Although you may not see <u>nobody</u> in the dark, it does not mean that <u>nobody</u> is there.**

    a.  The sentence is correct.

    b.  Although you may not see anyone in the dark, it does not mean that not nobody is there.

    c.  Although you may not see anyone in the dark, it does not mean that anyone is there.

    d.  Although you may not see nobody in the dark, it does not mean that not nobody is there.

**7. He <u>don't</u> have any money to buy clothes and neither <u>does</u> I.**

    a.  He doesn't have any money to buy clothes and neither do I.

    b.  He doesn't have any money to buy clothes and neither does I.

    c.  He don't have any money to buy clothes and neither do I.

    d. None of the choices are correct.

**8. Choose the sentence with the correct grammar.**

    a.  Because it really don't matter, I don't care if I go there.

    b.  Because it really doesn't matter, I doesn't care if I go there.

    c.  Because it really doesn't matter, I don't care if I go there.

    d.  Because it really don't matter, I don't care if I go there.

**9. When we go to the picnic, we will take potato salad and wieners.**

a.  None of the choices are correct.

b.  If you come to the picnic, bring potato salad and wieners.

c.  When we go to the picnic, we will bring potato salad and wieners.

d.  If you come to the picnic, take potato salad and wieners.

**10. The older children have already eat their dinner, but the baby has not yet ate anything.**

a. The older children have already eat their dinner, but the baby has not yet eaten anything.

b. The older children have already eaten their dinner, but the baby has not yet ate anything.

c. The older children have already eaten their dinner, but the baby has not yet eaten anything.

d. The sentence is correct.

**11. Newer cars use less gasoline, and produce less emissions.**

a.  Newer cars use fewer gasoline, and produce fewer emissions.

b.  None of the choices are correct.

c.  Newer cars use less gasoline, and produce fewer emissions.

d.  Newer cars fewer less gasoline, and produce less emissions.

**12. He should have <u>went</u> to the appointment; instead, he <u>gone</u> to the beach.**

    a.  He should have went to the appointment; instead, he went to the beach.

    b.  He should have gone to the appointment; instead, he went to the beach.

    c.  None of the choices are correct.

    d.  He should have gone to the appointment; instead, he gone to the beach.

**13. <u>However;</u> I believe that he didn't really try that hard.**

    a.  However, I believe that he didn't really try that hard.

    b.  However I believe that he didn't really try that hard.

    c.  None of the choices are correct.

    d.  However: I believe that he didn't really try that hard.

**14. It's important for you to know <u>it's</u> official name; <u>it's</u> called the Confederate Museum.**

    a. Its important for you to know its official name; its called the Confederate Museum.

    b. None of the choices are correct.

    c. It's important for you to know its official name; it's called the Confederate Museum.

    d. Its important for you to know it's official name; it's called the Confederate Museum.

**15. Once the chickens had laid their eggs, they laid on their nests to hatch them.**

    a. Once the chickens had layed their eggs, they lay on their nests to hatch them.

    b. Once the chickens had lay their eggs, they lay on their nests to hatch them.

    c. Once the chickens had laid their eggs, they lay on their nests to hatch them.

    d. None of the choices are correct.

**16. The mother <u>would not of punished</u> her daughter if she <u>could of avoided</u> it.**

    a. The mother would not of punished her daughter if she could have avoided it.

    b. The mother would not have punished her daughter if she could of avoided it.

    c. None of the choices are correct.

    d. The mother would not have punished her daughter if she could have avoided it.

**17. Even with <u>an</u> speed limit sign clearly posted, <u>a</u> inattentive driver may drive too fast.**

    a. Even with an speed limit sign clearly posted, an inattentive driver may drive too fast.

    b. Even with a speed limit sign clearly posted, a inattentive driver may drive too fast.

    c. None of the choices are correct.

    d. Even with a speed limit sign clearly posted, an inattentive driver may drive too fast.

**18. <u>Accept</u> for the roses, she did not <u>accept</u> John's frequent gifts.**

    a. Except for the roses, she did not accept John's frequent gifts.
    b. Accept for the roses, she did not except John's frequent gifts.
    c. None of the choices are correct.
    d. Except for the roses, she did not except John's frequent gifts.

**19. Although he continued to <u>advice</u> me, I no longer took his <u>advise</u>.**

    a. Although he continued to advise me, I no longer took his advice.
    b. Although he continued to advice me, I no longer took his advise.
    c. Although he continued to advise me, I no longer took his advise.
    d. None of the choices are correct.

**20. To <u>adopt</u> to the climate, we had to <u>adopt</u> a different style of clothing.**

    a. To adapt to the climate, we had to adapt a different style of clothing.

    b. To adopt to the climate, we had to adopt a different style of clothing.

    c. To adapt to the climate, we had to adopt a different style of clothing.

    d. None of the choices are correct.

**21.   When he's <u>between</u> friends, Robert seems confident, but, <u>between</u> you and me, he is really shy.**

    a. None of the choices are correct.

    b. When he's among friends, Robert seems confident, but, among you and me, he is really shy.

    c. When he's between friends, Robert seems confident, but, among you and me, he is really shy.

    d. When he's among friends, Robert seems confident, but, between you and me, he is really shy.

**22. I will be finished <u>at about</u> ten in the morning, and will be arriving at home <u>at</u> 6:30.**

    a. I will be finished at ten in the morning, and will be arriving at home at about 6:30.

    b. None of the choices are correct.

    c. I will be finished at about ten in the morning, and will be arriving at home at about 6:30.

    d. I will be finished at ten in the morning, and will be arriving at home at 6:30.

**23. <u>Beside</u> the red curtains and pillows, there was a red rug <u>besides</u> the couch.**

    a. Beside the red curtains and pillows, there was a red rug beside the couch.

    b. Besides the red curtains and pillows, there was a red rug beside the couch.

    c. Besides the red curtains and pillows, there was a red rug besides the couch.

    d. None of the choices are correct.

**24. Although John <u>may</u> swim very well, the lifeguard <u>may</u> not allow him to swim in the pool.**

    a. Although John can swim very well, the lifeguard may not allow him to swim in the pool.

    b. None of the choices are correct.

    c. Although John can swim very well, the lifeguard can not allow him to swim in the pool.

    d. Although John may swim very well, the lifeguard may not allow him to swim in the pool.

**25. Her <u>continuous</u> absences caused a <u>continuous</u> disruption at the office.**

    a. Her continuous absences caused a continual disruption at the office.

    b. Her continual absences caused a continuous disruption at the office.

    c. Her continual absences caused a continual disruption at the office.

    d. None of the choices are correct.

**26.  During the famine, the Irish people had to <u>immigrate</u> to other countries; many of them <u>immigrated</u> to the United States.**

    a. During the famine, the Irish people had to emigrate to other countries; many of them immigrated to the United States.

    b. None of the choices are correct.

    c. During the famine, the Irish people had to emigrate to other countries; many of them emigrated to the United States.

    d. During the famine, the Irish people had to immigrate to other countries; many of them emigrated to the United States.

**27. His home was <u>further</u> than we expected; <u>further</u>, the roads were very bad.**

    a. His home was farther than we expected; farther, the roads were very bad.

    b. His home was farther than we expected; further, the roads were very bad.

    c. None of the choices are correct.

    d. His home was further than we expected; farther, the roads were very bad.

**28. The volunteers brought groceries and toys to the homeless shelter; the latter was given to the staff, while the groceries were given directly to the children.**

    a. The volunteers brought groceries and toys to the homeless shelter; the latter were given to the staff, while the former were given directly to the children.

    b. The volunteers brought groceries and toys to the homeless shelter; the former was given to the staff, while the latter was given directly to the children.

    c. The volunteers brought groceries and toys to the homeless shelter; the groceries were given to the staff, while the former was given directly to the children.

    d. None of the choices are correct.

**29. You shouldn't <u>sit</u> in that chair wearing black pants; I <u>sit</u> the white cat there just a moment ago.**

    a. You shouldn't sit in that chair wearing black pants; I set the white cat there just a moment ago.

    b. You shouldn't set in that chair wearing black pants; I sit the white cat there just a moment ago.

    c. You shouldn't set in that chair wearing black pants; I set the white cat there just a moment ago.

    d. None of the choices are correct.

**30. Mars is the god of war.**

    a.   Mars is the god or war.
    b.   Mars is the God of war.
    c.   Mars is the God of War.
    d.   None of the choices are correct.

**31. This is her third term as <u>Mayor of chicago</u>.**

    a.   This is her third term as mayor of Chicago.
    b.   This is her third term as Mayor of Chicago.
    c.   This is her third term as mayor of chicago.
    d.   None of the above.

**32. I was able to speak with Susan Roberts <u>mayor of tampa</u>.**

    a. I was able to speak with Susan Roberts, Mayor of Tampa.

    b. I was able to speak with Susan Roberts, mayor of Tampa.

    c. I was able to speak with Susan Roberts, Mayor of tampa.

    d. None of the Above.

**33. I think <u>thanksgiving</u> is the best <u>Fall Holiday</u>.**

    a. I think thanksgiving is the best fall holiday.

    b. I think Thanksgiving is the best Fall holiday.

    c. I think Thanksgiving is the best fall holiday.

    d. None of the above.

**34.  I will be skipping The Fall 2013 semester.**

    a. I will be skipping the Fall 2013 Semester.

    b. I will be skipping the fall 2013 semester.

    c. I will be skipping the Fall 2013 semester.

    d. None of the above.

**35. The man was asked to come with <u>her</u> daughter and <u>his</u> test results.**

a. The man was asked to come with his daughter and her test results.

b. The man was asked to come with her daughter and her test results.

c. The man was asked to come with her daughter and our test results.

d. None of the above.

# ANSWER KEY

## SITUATIONAL JUDGEMENT

**1. B**

What has happened in the past is hard to reverse and instead of wasting more time, a  good leader would first, work towards meeting the requirements. In this given scenario, the possibility of incurring losses would be blamed on you. The best thing to do therefore is to brainstorm with Jackie and the rest of the team on what may be done by each member to meet the deadline.

Choices A, C and D will lead to resentment against the company and yourself and would be bad for moral.  The primary objective is to avoid loss and complete the project.   You can deal with other issues later.

**2. B**

Effective communication is two sided. Before you respond to the client's complaint, it is important to understand the complaint. Listen carefully and break down each important factor. Without proper listening, you are bound to misunderstand and irritate the client further. This way you end up losing clients. Be empathetic in your response and make yourself easy to understand.

Most people are naturally inclined to thinking that they are always correct in their thinking. This natural bias causes people to feel bad whenever they are proven wrong by someone. Choice A could seem appropriate, but it is detrimental to the future of the business. Most people blame everything on everyone but themselves. When you blame them, choice C, they are less likely to become loyal customers and your business loses in the long run. Choice D is obviously incorrect and can be eliminated right away.

## 3. D

Communication is very essential in any business undertaking. It is important to tell your side of the story as well as listen to deliberations by the team members. Consultations lead to better decision making.

Choice A seems appropriate; however, it fails to account for the supervisor's point of view or argument. However valid your argument might be, it is not sufficient to solve the issue. Going to work unwillingly (choice B) on the other hand is bad for you and for the company as well. You won't be able to concentrate and your productivity will be affected. Finding common ground or some type of accommodation is the best thing to do.

## 4. C

It is possible the supervisor is unaware of a policy. It therefore becomes important to speak with them politely. Rarely are supervisors wrong. However, sometimes unexpected things happen, but that does not allow you to do something you know violates company policy (Choice A). Declining to do the task (Choice B) without explanation is not likely to be taken well by your superior. Generally supervisors know the policies better than you although it is possible (Choice D). Choice C is the better choice.

## 5. B

Two heads are better than one. By allowing others to have an input in the final decision, you not only reduce unnecessary resistance but also increase employee commitment. To be effective, a leader should ensure team members are part of the decision-making process. Being involved gives them a sense of importance and belonging.

It is possible to make a thorough analysis of the factors involved in this and assume that one is able to make a decision that will be accepted by all (Choice A) however getting buy-in from everyone is a better strategy. Choices C and D are Obviously wrong choices and can be eliminated right away.

**6. D**

Some things are beyond your capacity as an employee, and above your pay-grade as they say. Whether it comes from the client or from other colleagues some issues need to be forwarded to the superiors. By directing Jane to your superiors you will have drawn a line in the chain of command. You will have presented the company with appropriate information for them to make an informed decision.

You cannot accept or refuse to meet the new demands from the client as you don't have the authority (choices B and C). Communicating in an official way is important for documentation purposes. By asking the client to write letters and email, (choice A) evidence for financial accounting is availed. However, it should not stop there.

**7. A**

Unless you first understand the viewpoint of your client, it will be very difficult to show them otherwise. By showing the client that you understand his problem, he is much more likely to agree with you at some point.

Unless you listen to the client, decoding his thoughts will be a great challenge to you (choice C). Choice B suggests a noble solution to the problem but fails to address the fundamental aspect of listening. Choice D is not an effective strategy - nobody like to be told they are wrong.

**8. B**

Involving a neutral person (the supervisor) in conflict resolution leads to better understanding and chance of resolution. By involving a third party, you can diffuse the situation quickly and amicably. The leader offers proper guidance and issues directions to safeguard the interests of the organization.
It is not a sure thing that issuing an apology would bring to an end of the conflict (choice A) – more than that is required. Similarly choice C, is not a solution,  as it may be taken as an accusation.

**9. B**

Asking for collaboration from others gives you a better chance to analyze the situation and make the best decision.

It also makes them feel valued which raises their commitment levels.

Choice A is good, but choice B, asking for collaboration is better. Choices C and D, taking action without information, is dangerous to the business. It is similar to driving a car blindfolded. It is hard to make the right call when faced with a new challenge. Making decisions under pressure is a challenge to most leaders. Chances of error are so high that consulting is not an option but a necessity.

## 10. A
Work-related conflict should be resolved by higher authority. An independent supervisor can provide the appropriate direction.

Choice D, discussing as a team and asking for solutions could deteriorate with members taking sides. Involve only the right people while solving such specific problems. Choice C, talking to each separately, may resolve but you are taking a chance you will not be able to resolve. Bringing it to you superiors is the best choice (choice A). Choice B, offering unsolicited advice would not be appreciated or resolve the situation.

## 11. B
The editor is your boss and that's the way things are so if they are not happy that will mean some adjustment on your part. However, if you feel the editor is being unreasonable, you may want to talk with them. Choice C, referring to the company policy document is a possibility depending on the situation. However choice B is the better choice.

Choice A, ignorance is no defense in any situation in life. By ignoring to address the concerns of the clients you set a pace for failure. You are bound to lose more clients. Choice D, blaming the supervisor will only lead to more complications. Building resentment and bad publicity are sure consequences of such behavior.

## 12. A
Division of labor and specialization are the best ways of solving increasing workload. This gives the employees equal time

to work on given tasks to ease the workload. Division of labor promotes innovation and invention and increases output per employee.

Choice B, may be a good idea, however management very likely has limited options to help. Choice C, asking for higher pay doesn't solve the problem. Choice D, may be a good option if, and only if all else fails.

## 13. B

You are nominally in charge so it falls on you to handle the situation. However, you can't do much about the line-up. Choice B, ask for patience for a bit longer is the best choice.

Choice A, offering incentives may be considered later depending on how long you wait. Choice C, and D don't do anything to diffuse the situation.

## 14. B

Life is a sequence of lessons that start from childhood and continues in adulthood. By learning from one's mistake, you are likely to improve next time. Sometimes we succeed and sometimes we learn. Failure is a part of life and we all should embrace failure as a lesson for a better tomorrow. It may be necessary to discuss the failure and learnings with your supervisor.

Choices A, C and D do not addresses the core issue.

## 15. A

First, discuss it with your colleague. There may be things you are not aware of preventing them from getting information to you quickly. If this doesn't work, go to the other options.

Choice B, going to your supervisor is an option for later. Choice C, is not a great approach. Making demands is not likely to change anything. Choice D, getting information from other sources would mean that there is a disharmony between the key participants. This may be an option for later or as a last resort.

## 16. D

The changes are going to continue so your choice is to resist (difficult) or become more involved. Once you are more involved in why the changes are taking place they become easier to manage.

## 17. A

Making sure everyone understands the goals of the project gets everyone on board is the first step.

Choice B, discriminating against team members will alienate them. Asking for assistance, choice B, from others is a necessity but comes after being clear on goals and obtaining feedback. Choice D, declining assistance is not a good strategy to start.

## 18. A

A straightforward and direct approach is best. Sugar coating or avoiding the bad news will come back on you.

Choices B and C, avoiding the issue and blaming others will cause problems later. Choice C, getting others to related bad news will also cause problems later.

## 19. B

The aspect of monitoring carries the weight in this scenario. Unregulated competition could lead to unethical behaviors. Competition is healthy in any business and human encounters. By regulating the competition, the goals are likely to be met easily.

Choice A, discouraging competition loses the benefits of competition. Competition is healthy provided limits are defined and observed. Choice D, is a good choice but choice A is better. Offering a reward may come later.

## 20. D

Self-improvement is a continuous process and any person who can't handle feedback or criticism positively loses the opportunity to improve.

Choice A and C, retaliating against your critics or resenting, is destructive. You can't win an argument and even when you think you have, the resentment stirred in your victim works against you and your plans. Choice B, giving the matter to supervisors, may be a next step but not a good strategy initially.

### 21. B

Finding and correctly matching the strengths of the individual team members with those needed in the business is the most appropriate course of action. Performance analysis will assist you in determining which employee fits which position and assigning them duties in those areas.

Choices A and B, discarding or replacing members of the team and replacing would be time consuming.

### 22. C

Clear communication is vital in such a scenario as a first step. If this doesn't resolve the issue the other choices are next steps.

Being bossy (choice B) leads to resentment. Choice D, requesting their supervisor intervene is a possible next step.

### 23. C

Unless you are able to understand the reason behind the disagreement, you will not be in a position to accomplish much. By taking time to break down the details of the disagreement the chances of reaching a consensus are higher.

Terminating the employee (choice A) does not benefit the company. Choice B, disciplining is an option for later. Choice D suggests for a complete overhaul of the initial plan.

### 24. A

Team members need clear communication to assimilating the changes. This approach ensures that none of the team members are left behind and everyone participates mapping out the changes.

New information is to be considered and deliberated on to avoid misunderstandings. Abruptly changing or disregarding the facts will not succeed (Choices B and D). Choice C, consulting others may be necessary as a next stop.

### 25. C

Be objective in finding a common ground with the employee. Base your argument on facts and consider both sides of the story. Don't make accusations.

Choices A, B and D, over-ruling, rebuking or disciplining may be necessary but not as a first step.

## 26. C

Listening is the key to assist the client. This way you have a chance of understanding the concerns raised by the client. You will also be in a better position to close a sale.

Choice A, referring the client to another agent, you have lost the client and possibly their friends and relatives. You reduce their level of confidence in you and your company. Choice D, repeating what has been happening is also not likely to be of help to the client. Choice B, refusing the client may be an option if the issues are too difficult, but not as a first step.

## 27. A

Verbal communication is not always the best because there is never proof of communication. The best way to communicate is through written communication. By following written communication, you are provided with evidence of communication for reference in future.

Choice B, refusing to consider verbal communication is too extreme. Choice D is incorrect because you don't want to be complacent when communicating with others.

## 28. C

Some of the disagreements require input from higher authority. Supervisors are in a better position to resolve a conflict between junior employees.

Choice A is not a resolution. Choice B, confronting the behavior may work if done properly, but could also make the situation worse, however, choice C is the better choice. Choice D, motivating yourself could work towards making you feel better but not towards resolving the conflict.

## 29. B

Choice B is the best choice. Being hospitable and polite is key.

Directing the client to other unknown offices could confuse him and you miss an opportunity.  Choice C, finding the right information may seem a good choice, however, the client should be referred to an expert and knowledgeable person.

## 30. C
Clear communication is the best choice.

Choice B, taking this matter to the authority may make a person appear incompetent and unable to handle simple situations. Choice D is incorrect since customer satisfaction should always be a top concern.

## 31. A
By motivating him, you positively impact the results. Everyone needs a pat in the back and a person to motivate them when tough times comes.

Choice B, informing the supervisors, might not be the most appropriate thing to do, at least at first. As a colleague, its incorrect to do absolutely nothing (choice D). If motivating fails, you may then suggest counseling sessions (choice C).

## 32. A
The first impression is important in human encounters because it lasts through the duration the people get to interact. Good posture and clothing are indicators of success and the clients are likely to trust you more.

Choice C, dramatizing your idea does not necessarily mean that you create a good first impression.  Choices B and D, ignoring the advice is no solution.

## 33. D
By identifying the key issues of discontent, both of you are likely to forge a better way. It must be well accommodated by both parties for lasting solutions.

Choice A, requesting cooperation doesn't mean you will get it. Choice C, involving the manager, is too soon.

**34. B**

We all get bored easily by routine. By finding new tasks to engage, you trick the brain in staying active for longer periods of time.

Winners never quit, that is the basic principle in any form of business. As an employee, you shouldn't focus on getting a simpler job. Instead, your main focus should be on building capacity to withstand and overcome challenges.

**35. A**

Introducing incentives is likely to motivate your team members.

Choice B, reducing compensation is likely to alienating. Choice C, talking about the need to be committed could easily come across as talking down.

**36. A**

Complimenting him in public, you motivate other employees to do better. This is a sure way to increase their level of commitment to the success of the business.

Choice B, demeaning others will reduce moral and motivation.  Choice C, emailing may be the only option under some circumstances but not the best.

**37. A**

Regular meetings keep everyone up-to-date to discuss issues, potential improvements and in touch with each other.

Choice B will not help. Choice C, selecting the best team players, means re-making the whole team – only as a last resort.  Choice D, becoming more involved is good advice, but choice A is better.

**38. B**

If you want the best, you need to become the best. By working longer hours, you encourage your team members.

Choice A is good, but choice B is better because it is more visible.  Everyone will you arriving early and leaving late. Lecturing or condemning, choices C and D, never helps.

## 39. B

Making clear to the team the deadlines and what is expected of them is the first step.

Choice C is a good suggestion, if there is an issue with some parts of the project.

## 40. B

Making clear to the team the deadlines and what is expected so everyone knows where they stand.

Choice A, keeping a monopoly of information is likely to cause chaos and lead to disruption. Working three times harder, choice C, however effective it may sound, is equally ineffective.

# SENTENCE ORDER

## 1. E B C A D

Sentence E is first because it explains why movies are so scary to make. Sentence B continues talking about the ideas and two of the important people who are involved. Sentence C has to come next, because A refers back to it. Sentence D finishes the paragraph by referring to the people and the frightening aspect of making a movie.

## 2. B E D A C

Sentence B provides a little history about how easy it was to spot crocodiles. Sentence E explains what is going on NOW. Sentence D includes a reason why crocodiles are disappearing, which fits well after Sentence E. Sentence A explains why nothing is being done. Sentence C support the information in Sentence A.

## 3. A E C B D

Sentence A needs to come first because it discusses the first use of crowd-funding. Sentence E continues the information about Pulitzer's work. Sentence C transitions to a new time period. Sentence B talks about the platforms online. Sentence D discusses what project creators need to do when they are online.

**4. E C D A B**

Sentence E is first because is gives background information on the Choco Pie. Sentence C is next because of the chronology of the paragraph. Sentence D moves to the next step in chronological order. Sentence A continues to talk about Orion. Finally, sentence B explains what is happening now.

**5. C E A B D**

Sentence C generally explains the number of steps. Sentence E uses the word "first" to designate its place in the process. Sentence A needs to come after E to make sense. Sentence B includes the second separate step. Sentence D is the final step.

# READING

**1. 1. A**

The correct answer because that fact is stated directly in the passage. The passage explains that Anne taught Helen to hear by allowing her to feel the vibrations in her throat.

**2. D**

This question tests the reader's summarization skills. The question is asking very generally about the message of the passage, and the title, "Ways Characters Communicate in Theatre," is one indication of that. The other choices A, B, and C are all directly from the text, and therefore readers may be inclined to select one of them, but are too specific to encapsulate the entirety of the passage and its message.

**3. C**

This question tests the reader's summarization skills. The use of the word "actually" in describing what kind of people poets are, as well as other moments like this, may lead readers to selecting Choices B or D, but the author is more information than trying to persuade readers. The author gives no indication that she loves poetry (choice B) or that people, students specifically (D), should write poems. Choice A is incorrect because the style and content of this paragraph do not match those of a foreword; forewords usually focus on the history or ideas of a specific poem to introduce it more fully and help it stand out against other poems. The author here focuses on several poems and gives broad statements. Instead, she tells a kind of story about poems, giving three very broad time periods in which to discuss them, thereby giving a brief history of poetry, as choice C states.

### 4. A
This question tests the reader's summarization skills. Key words in the topic sentences of each of the paragraphs ("oldest," "Renaissance," "modern") should give the reader an idea that the author is moving chronologically. The opening and closing sentence-paragraphs are broad and talk generally. B seems reasonable, but epic poems are mentioned in two paragraphs, eliminating the idea that only new types of poems are used in each paragraph. Choice C is also easily eliminated because the author clearly mentions several different poets, groups of people, and poems. Choice D also seems reasonable, considering that the author does move from older forms of poetry to newer forms, but use of "so (that)" makes this statement false, for the author gives no indication that she is rushing (the paragraphs are about the same size) or that she prefers modern poetry.

### 5. D
This question tests the reader's attention to detail. The key word is "invented"--it ties together the Mesopotamians, who invented the written word, and the fact that they, as the inventors, also invented and used poetry. The other selections focus on other details mentioned in the passage, such as that the Renaissance's admiration of the Greeks (choice C) and that Beowulf is in Old English (choice A). Choice B may seem like an attractive answer because it is unlike the others and because the idea of heroes seems rooted in ancient and early civilizations.

### 6. B
This question tests the reader's vocabulary and contextualization skills. "Telling" is not an unusual word, but it may be used here in a way that is not familiar to readers, as an adjective rather than a verb in gerund form. A may seem like the obvious answer to a reader looking for a verb to match

the use they are familiar with. If the reader understands that the word is being used as an adjective and that choice A is a ploy, they may opt to select choice D, "wordy," but it does not make sense in context. Choice C can be easily eliminated, and doesn't have any connection to the paragraph or passage. "Significant" (choice B) makes sense contextually, especially relative to the phrase "give insight" used later in the sentence.

# CORRECTING SENTENCES

### 7. D
Suggested revision of sentence 1, "Humankind's thirst for knowledge is insatiable, making curiosity a driving force for advances throughout history."

Use the gender neutral "humankind. Replace the past perfect "has always been" with the present tense to make a simpler and more direct sentence. "Though history" is incorrect. Use "throughout" when referring to a time period. Replace the preposition "for" with "in."

### 8. A

Sentence 6 is the least relevant. "Curiosity was launched in late November 2011 from Cape Canaveral Air Force Station in Florida."

The third paragraph talks about the objectives of the rover. All sentences other than sentence 7 mention the objectives. This sentence, however, informs about when the spacecraft was launched.

### 9. A
Sentence 10 is least relevant to the main idea of the third paragraph. The following changes are suggested, "<u>To achieve its goals</u>, Curiosity has been engineered with cutting-edge technologies worth a budgetary expense exceeding 2.5 billion US dollars."

Clearly, the last paragraph talks about how Curiosity has been engineered to accomplish its objectives. The previous paragraph addressing the objectives of the rover, addition of the phrase "To achieve its goals," in choice A, acts as a transition sentence between the paragraphs.

## 10. D

The changes needed to sentence 5 are, "So far, NASA has carried out several exploratory missions to Mars and the rover robot "Curiosity" is the latest and most sophisticated of all."

"Curiosity" is the name of a spacecraft that was assigned the particular name because of its association of its mission to satisfy our curiosity about the planet Mars. In this respect, the name bears a special meaning and emphasis, which must be reflected in representing it using the quotation mark.

Use of the adjective "exploratory" to describe the missions is correct.

Choice D offers these changes.

## 11. C

Sentence 11 is a fragment. "The discovery is significant because so far, no attempt has been made to use the abundant infrared radiation we receive throughout the year."

The fragment contains a subordinate clause derived from the complete thought "The discovery is significant because so far no attempt has been made to make use of the infra-red radiation that we receive in an abundant supply throughout the year." It also contains the subject of the main clause, "The discovery," but does not have any verbal phrase for the main clause. Since the main clause remains incomplete, the thought is expressed in part. Therefore, it is a sentence fragment.

## 12. C

Sentence 9 can be deleted to reduce redundancy. "This is a major discovery in the solar power generation industry as it offers a cheap source of harnessing the Sun's energy."

Sentence 9 contributes to double redundancy; that is, it repeats two separate ideas. Along with repeating the cost-effective characteristic of the new discovery, it also reiterates the fact that it is a major discovery, both of which are unnecessary. It also interferes in the paragraph transition which can be established between sentence 8 and 10 if it is removed.

## 13. B

Suggested corrections to sentence 10, "Oleic acid, the main ingredient of olive oil, absorbs infra-red radiation, which is the major component of the Sun's radiation reaching the Earth."

The sentence is missing the subordinate conjunction "which" or "that" necessary to construct the subordinate clause, with a comma before "which."  Choices B and C suggest these changes, but since choice C contains a punctuation error, only B is has the valid answer.

## 14. D

Suggested changes to sentence 2, "With continued concern over global climate change, environmentalists are urging governments to lower their dependence on fossil fuels to en-sure reduced carbon emission into the atmosphere."

This sentence contains inappropriate use of gerunds and infinitives. To-infinitives are preferred when the continuous form of a main verb is used right before or after them. Here,, "urging" should be followed by the to-infinitive of "lower." Further across the sentence, the linking phrase "to," has only one acceptable form; itself. Therefore, the verb which is linked to must contain the infinitive form. The gerund form must be discarded. The only valid choice is D.

## 15. B

Suggested changes to sentence 6 are, "This information, coupled with conventional on-site procedures, help archae-ologists plan their excavation carefully and efficiently."

The second paragraph points out the significance of satel-lite imaging for archeological studies. The original sentence only makes a general claim. Choice A contradicts excavation principles by adding "along with a supply of heavy machin-ery" which would destroy the site. Choice B, more appropri-ately, adds the aspects of archeological excavation that are going to be boosted by the technology. Choices C and D offer very little relevance to satellite imaging and the dimensions of excavation that are going to be affected.

## 16. C

 Sentence 9 can be re-written, "Different points in a civiliza-tion reflect IR radiation differently, provide detailed insight about the causes of these differing heat signatures."

This is a shorter and more concise sentence which eliminates some details.

### 17. A

The following sentence, inserted after sentence 3, would best illustrate the main idea, "The application has inspired archaeologists to use it for searching for the traces of ancient civilizations and other anthropological dynamics."

Choice A points out the significance of the application with some details that are addressed in the subsequent paragraphs. All other choices are either too general or less relevant to the main idea of the passage.

### 18. A

Suggested changes to sentence 4 are, "The key feature of the new tool- according to Professor Sarah Parcak, who discovered many cities, temples and pyramids covered under sands and sediment- is that it offers a wider perspective in size and scale of the location."

The changes in this sentence are related to punctuation. The original sentence contains a semicolon before a verbal phrase which is not justifiable with its standard use. The sentence can be modified using parenthetic dashes since using parenthetic commas makes the sentence very complicated as the sentence contains several clauses and a list.

### 19. D

Sentence 13 is not consistent with the author's purpose. "In the process, she somehow managed to uphold the courage to address the issues facing education for girls and proposed solutions for them."

This sentence, ironically contrasts the character of the passage, and in a way belittles Malala's efforts to address the issues facing girls education, particularly with the words "somehow," "managed" and "uphold." This is, to a great extent, inconsistent with the author's appreciation of Malala.

### 20. C

Suggested changes to sentence 10 to focus attention on the main idea are, "Inspired by her father, who is an professional educator himself, she decided to work for the education and establishment of girls in her locality, Mingora, a suburban town in Swat District."

The second paragraph discusses the challenges facing Malala and  young girls like her. It fine-tunes the reason why Malala had to change her ambition even though she is a talented and successful student; showing that she actually did not give up on her ambition, but rather sacrificed it for materializing others'. In this sense, her father was a role model from whom she could receive inspiration only; not persuasion, instruction or contradiction- for making up her mind to be an professional educator like him. Therefore, choices A, B and D are not relevant. Choice C focuses on the main idea.

# VOCABULARY

**1. C**
**Dauntless:** adj. Invulnerable to fear or intimidation.

**2. A**
**Juxtaposed:** adj. Placed side-by-side often for comparison or contrast.

**3. B**
**Regicide:** v. killing of a king.

**4. A**
**Pernicious:** adj. Causing much harm in a subtle way.

**5. A**
**Immune:** adj. Resistant to a particular infection or toxin owing to the presence of specific antibodies.

**6. B**
**Nimble:** adj. Quick and light in movement or action.

**7. A**
**Queries:** n. Questions or inquiries.

**8. C**
**Depose:** To remove (a leader) from (high) office, without killing the incumbent.

**9. D**
**Pedestrian:** Ordinary, dull; everyday; unexceptional.

**10. B**
**Petulant:** adj. Childishly irritable.

**11. D**
**Pesticide:** n. A substance used for destroying insects or other organisms harmful to cultivated plants or to animals.

**12. D**
**Salient:** adj. worthy or note or relevant.

**13. B**
**Sedentary:** adj. not moving or sitting in one place.

**14. A**
**Famine:** n. extreme scarcity of food.

**15. A**
**Stint:** n. To be sparing.

**16. A**
**Precipitate:** v. to rain.

**17. C**
**Edify:** v. To instruct or improve morally or intellectually.

**18. B**
**Egress:** n. An exit or way out.

**19. A**
**Recede:** v. To move back, to move away.

**20. A**
**Confidential:** adj. kept secret within a certain circle of persons; not intended to be known publicly.

# ENGLISH LANGUAGE ARTS

## 1. C
Comma separate phrases.

## 2. D
The comma separates clauses and numbers are separated with a comma.  The correct sentence is,
'To travel around the globe, you have to drive 25,000 miles.'

## 3. A
The dog loved chasing bones, but never ate them; it was running that he enjoyed.

## 4. B
The semicolon links independent clauses with a conjunction (therefore).

## 5. D
The third conditional is used for talking about an unreal situation (that did not happen) in the past.  For example, "If I had studied harder, [if clause] I would have passed the exam [main clause].  Which is the same as, "I failed the exam, because I didn't study hard enough."

## 6. C
Double negative sentence.  In double negative sentences, one negative is replaced with "any."

## 7. A
Disagreeing with a negative statement uses "neither." Disagreeing with a negative statement uses "neither." Use "I do" and "He does."

## 8. C
Doesn't, does not, or does is used with the third person singular--words like he, she, and it. Don't, do not, or do is used for other subjects.

## 9. C
Bring vs. Take.  Usage depends on your location. Something coming your way is brought to you. Something going away is taken from you.

## 10. C

Present perfect. You cannot use the Present Perfect with specific time expressions such as: yesterday, one year ago, last week, when I was a child, at that moment, that day, one day, etc. The Present Perfect is used with unspecific expressions such as: ever, never, once, many times, several times, before, so far, already, yet, etc.

## 11. C

Fewer vs. Less. 'Fewer' is used with countables and 'less' is used with uncountables.

## 12. B

Went vs. Gone. Went is the simple past tense. Gone is used in the past perfect.

## 13. A

When using 'however,' place a comma before and after, except when however begins the sentence.

## 14. C

Its vs. It's. 'It's' is a contraction for it is or it has. 'Its' is a possessive pronoun meaning, more or less, of it or belonging to it.

## 15. C

Lay vs. Lie. Lie requires an object and lay does not. Laid is the past tense of lay.

## 16. D

The third conditional is used for talking about an unreal situation (that did not happen) in the past. For example, "If I had studied harder, [if clause] I would have passed the exam [main clause]. Which is the same as, "I failed the exam, because I didn't study hard enough."

## 17. D

A vs. An. The article 'a' come before a consonant and 'an' comes before a vowel.

## 18. A

Accept vs. Except. To accept is to receive or to say yes. Except is a preposition that means excluding.

**19. A**
Advise vs. Advice. To advise is to give advice.   Advice is an opinion that someone offers.

**20. C**
Adapt vs. Adopt.
Adapt means "to change." Usually we adapt to someone or something. Adopt means "to take as one's own."

**21. D**
Among vs. Between.  'Among' is for more than 2 items, and 'between' is only for 2 items.

When he's among friends (many or more than 2), Robert seems confident, but, between you and me (two), he is very shy.

**22. D**
At vs. About.  At refers to a specific time and about refers to a more general time.  A common usage is 'at about 10,' but it isn't proper grammar.

**23. B**
Beside vs. Besides.  'Beside' means next to, and 'besides' means in addition to.

**24. A**
Can vs. May.  'Can' refers to ability and 'may' refers to permission.

Although John can swim (is able to. very well, he may not (permission) be allowed to swim in the pool.

**25. B**
Continual vs. Continuous.  'Continuous' means a time with no interruption and 'continual' means a time with interruption.

Her continual absences (with interruption – not always absent) caused a continuous disruption (the disruption was ongoing without interruption) at the office.

**26. A**
Emigrate vs. Immigrate.  To emigrate means to leave one's country and to immigrate means to come to a country.

**27. B**

Further vs. Farther.  'Farther' is used for physical distance, and 'further' is used for figurative distance.

**28. B**

Former vs. Latter.  'Former' refers to the first of two things, 'latter' to the second.

**29. A**

Sit vs. Set.  'Set' requires an object – something to set down. 'Sit' is something that you do, like sit on the chair.

**30. C**

The names of God, specific deities, religious figures, and holy books are capitalized.

**31. B**

Capitalize a title when used with a name or other noun.  So, The Mayor of Chicago is capitalized, whereas "he spoke to the mayor" is not.

**32. B**

Titles preceding names are capitalized, but not titles that follow names.

**33. C**

Holidays are capitalized, the names of seasons are not.

**34. C**

The names of seasons are not capitalized because they are generic nouns.  If a season is used in a title, such as the "Fall 2012 semester," Fall 2012 is a title and capitalized.

**35. A**

A Pronoun should conform to its antecedent in gender, number and person.

# PRACTICE TEST
# QUESTIONS SET 2

THE PRACTICE TEST PORTION PRESENTS QUESTIONS THAT ARE REPRESENTATIVE OF THE TYPE OF QUESTION YOU SHOULD EXPECT TO FIND ON THE CORRECTIONS OFFICER EXAM. HOWEVER, THEY ARE NOT INTENDED TO MATCH EXACTLY WHAT IS ON THE EXAM.

For the best results, take this Practice Test as if it were the real exam. Set aside time when you will not be disturbed, and a location that is quiet and free of distractions. Read the instructions carefully, read each question carefully, and answer to the best of your ability.

Use the bubble answer sheets provided. When you have completed the Practice Test, check your answer against the Answer Key and read the explanation provided.

# SITUATIONAL JUDGEMENT

|     | A | B | C | D | E |     | A | B | C | D | E |
| --- | - | - | - | - | - | --- | - | - | - | - | - |
| 1   | ○ | ○ | ○ | ○ | ○ | 21  | ○ | ○ | ○ | ○ | ○ |
| 2   | ○ | ○ | ○ | ○ | ○ | 22  | ○ | ○ | ○ | ○ | ○ |
| 3   | ○ | ○ | ○ | ○ | ○ | 23  | ○ | ○ | ○ | ○ | ○ |
| 4   | ○ | ○ | ○ | ○ | ○ | 24  | ○ | ○ | ○ | ○ | ○ |
| 5   | ○ | ○ | ○ | ○ | ○ | 25  | ○ | ○ | ○ | ○ | ○ |
| 6   | ○ | ○ | ○ | ○ | ○ | 26  | ○ | ○ | ○ | ○ | ○ |
| 7   | ○ | ○ | ○ | ○ | ○ | 27  | ○ | ○ | ○ | ○ | ○ |
| 8   | ○ | ○ | ○ | ○ | ○ | 28  | ○ | ○ | ○ | ○ | ○ |
| 9   | ○ | ○ | ○ | ○ | ○ | 29  | ○ | ○ | ○ | ○ | ○ |
| 10  | ○ | ○ | ○ | ○ | ○ | 30  | ○ | ○ | ○ | ○ | ○ |
| 11  | ○ | ○ | ○ | ○ | ○ | 31  | ○ | ○ | ○ | ○ | ○ |
| 12  | ○ | ○ | ○ | ○ | ○ | 32  | ○ | ○ | ○ | ○ | ○ |
| 13  | ○ | ○ | ○ | ○ | ○ | 33  | ○ | ○ | ○ | ○ | ○ |
| 14  | ○ | ○ | ○ | ○ | ○ | 34  | ○ | ○ | ○ | ○ | ○ |
| 15  | ○ | ○ | ○ | ○ | ○ | 35  | ○ | ○ | ○ | ○ | ○ |
| 16  | ○ | ○ | ○ | ○ | ○ | 36  | ○ | ○ | ○ | ○ | ○ |
| 17  | ○ | ○ | ○ | ○ | ○ | 37  | ○ | ○ | ○ | ○ | ○ |
| 18  | ○ | ○ | ○ | ○ | ○ | 38  | ○ | ○ | ○ | ○ | ○ |
| 19  | ○ | ○ | ○ | ○ | ○ | 39  | ○ | ○ | ○ | ○ | ○ |
| 20  | ○ | ○ | ○ | ○ | ○ | 40  | ○ | ○ | ○ | ○ | ○ |

## SENTENCE ORDER

1. ___  ___  ___  ___  ___  ___

2. ___  ___  ___  ___  ___  ___

3. ___  ___  ___  ___  ___  ___

4. ___  ___  ___  ___  ___  ___

5. ___  ___  ___  ___  ___  ___

# Reading and Sentence Correction

|     | A | B | C | D |
|-----|---|---|---|---|
| 1   | ○ | ○ | ○ | ○ |
| 2   | ○ | ○ | ○ | ○ |
| 3   | ○ | ○ | ○ | ○ |
| 4   | ○ | ○ | ○ | ○ |
| 5   | ○ | ○ | ○ | ○ |
| 6   | ○ | ○ | ○ | ○ |
| 7   | ○ | ○ | ○ | ○ |
| 8   | ○ | ○ | ○ | ○ |
| 9   | ○ | ○ | ○ | ○ |
| 10  | ○ | ○ | ○ | ○ |
| 11  | ○ | ○ | ○ | ○ |
| 12  | ○ | ○ | ○ | ○ |
| 13  | ○ | ○ | ○ | ○ |
| 14  | ○ | ○ | ○ | ○ |
| 15  | ○ | ○ | ○ | ○ |
| 16  | ○ | ○ | ○ | ○ |
| 17  | ○ | ○ | ○ | ○ |
| 18  | ○ | ○ | ○ | ○ |
| 19  | ○ | ○ | ○ | ○ |
| 20  | ○ | ○ | ○ | ○ |

## VOCABULARY

|  | A | B | C | D |
|---|---|---|---|---|
| 1 | ○ | ○ | ○ | ○ |
| 2 | ○ | ○ | ○ | ○ |
| 3 | ○ | ○ | ○ | ○ |
| 4 | ○ | ○ | ○ | ○ |
| 5 | ○ | ○ | ○ | ○ |
| 6 | ○ | ○ | ○ | ○ |
| 7 | ○ | ○ | ○ | ○ |
| 8 | ○ | ○ | ○ | ○ |
| 9 | ○ | ○ | ○ | ○ |
| 10 | ○ | ○ | ○ | ○ |
| 11 | ○ | ○ | ○ | ○ |
| 12 | ○ | ○ | ○ | ○ |
| 13 | ○ | ○ | ○ | ○ |
| 14 | ○ | ○ | ○ | ○ |
| 15 | ○ | ○ | ○ | ○ |
| 16 | ○ | ○ | ○ | ○ |
| 17 | ○ | ○ | ○ | ○ |
| 18 | ○ | ○ | ○ | ○ |
| 19 | ○ | ○ | ○ | ○ |
| 20 | ○ | ○ | ○ | ○ |

# ENGLISH GRAMMAR

|    | A | B | C | D | E |    | A | B | C | D | E |
|----|---|---|---|---|---|----|---|---|---|---|---|
| 1  | ○ | ○ | ○ | ○ | ○ | 21 | ○ | ○ | ○ | ○ | ○ |
| 2  | ○ | ○ | ○ | ○ | ○ | 22 | ○ | ○ | ○ | ○ | ○ |
| 3  | ○ | ○ | ○ | ○ | ○ | 23 | ○ | ○ | ○ | ○ | ○ |
| 4  | ○ | ○ | ○ | ○ | ○ | 24 | ○ | ○ | ○ | ○ | ○ |
| 5  | ○ | ○ | ○ | ○ | ○ | 25 | ○ | ○ | ○ | ○ | ○ |
| 6  | ○ | ○ | ○ | ○ | ○ | 26 | ○ | ○ | ○ | ○ | ○ |
| 7  | ○ | ○ | ○ | ○ | ○ | 27 | ○ | ○ | ○ | ○ | ○ |
| 8  | ○ | ○ | ○ | ○ | ○ | 28 | ○ | ○ | ○ | ○ | ○ |
| 9  | ○ | ○ | ○ | ○ | ○ | 29 | ○ | ○ | ○ | ○ | ○ |
| 10 | ○ | ○ | ○ | ○ | ○ | 30 | ○ | ○ | ○ | ○ | ○ |
| 11 | ○ | ○ | ○ | ○ | ○ | 31 | ○ | ○ | ○ | ○ | ○ |
| 12 | ○ | ○ | ○ | ○ | ○ | 32 | ○ | ○ | ○ | ○ | ○ |
| 13 | ○ | ○ | ○ | ○ | ○ | 33 | ○ | ○ | ○ | ○ | ○ |
| 14 | ○ | ○ | ○ | ○ | ○ | 34 | ○ | ○ | ○ | ○ | ○ |
| 15 | ○ | ○ | ○ | ○ | ○ | 35 | ○ | ○ | ○ | ○ | ○ |
| 16 | ○ | ○ | ○ | ○ | ○ | 36 | ○ | ○ | ○ | ○ | ○ |
| 17 | ○ | ○ | ○ | ○ | ○ | 37 | ○ | ○ | ○ | ○ | ○ |
| 18 | ○ | ○ | ○ | ○ | ○ | 38 | ○ | ○ | ○ | ○ | ○ |
| 19 | ○ | ○ | ○ | ○ | ○ | 39 | ○ | ○ | ○ | ○ | ○ |
| 20 | ○ | ○ | ○ | ○ | ○ | 40 | ○ | ○ | ○ | ○ | ○ |

## 1. Scenario

As a department head, you propose new procedure and you are sure it will improve the work process. Some of the employee in the department oppose it. One of your subordinates criticizes the procedure to your direct boss.

What action should you take?

a. You choose not to respond to prevent the situation to escalating into a conflict.

b. You punish that person for skipping protocol and going to your boss and work to promote the idea more enthusiastically.

c. You invite the employee for a discussion and explain to him that bypassing your authority cannot be tolerated.

d. You decide to keep your employees satisfied by implementing the idea in part to maintain the employees trust in you as their manager.

## 2. Scenario

At a strategy meeting with your direct supervisor and the marketing manager, your find yourself in the middle of a conflict between them. You understand that the two are always in constant conflict and do not go along professionally. They are asking you to pick a side about the strategies for a new campaign.

What should you do?

a. You go with the marketing managers idea since she is senior it would be safer and politically wiser to support her as she has more influence on the future of your career.

b. You accept your supervisor's idea since he is directly above you and directly influences your daily routine which makes it politically correct to side with him.

c. You measure the advantages and disadvantages of both sides and make a decision without getting involved in their personal conflict.

d.  You believe that choosing a side will negatively impact your career since both sides are superior to you. You refuse to pick a side and say both strategies are equally successful.

## 3. Scenario

After serving two years as the sales manager, the director appoints a new deputy manager. You however find her disloyal and arrogant in many ways. You discover the director is considering an opportunity for her in a different position after this. The downside, is this would speed up her promotion.

What should you do?

a.  Since the course would lead to her relocation, you encourage and approve her participation in the course.

b.  You contact your director and recommend she be relocated to another position best suited to her capabilities.

c.  You approve her participation and take time to discuss it with her. You honestly express your concerns and work out your differences and update your director.

d.  You blindly approve her participation since it was offered by the director. You voice your concerns to the director separately.

## 4. Scenario

For the past year you have worked as a salesperson and have consistently hit sales targets. Recently, for personal reasons you haven't been focused and haven't been making sales targets. Changes in the market are also a factor, decreasing your sales by a significant margin. Your director does not seem to understand the changes in the market and is blaming you for the reduction in sales figures.

What should you do?

a. Talk to your director about your personal situation and apologize for the decline in the team's performance. Request for a few days off to put your house in order.

b. You decide to put your personal issues aside and consult other sales directors on how they deal with a volatile market. You fully dedicate yourself to your work.

c. You update your director on the market changes. You explain to him that changing or improving sales with the current conditions is beyond your ability.

d. You decide to put pressure on your team scolding them for the poor performance. You go ahead and set new targets with the market changes in mind.

## 5. Scenario

You have been working at the same company for three years and have successfully risen through the ranks. You now have the feeling that you have reached your potential in the company and start pursuing options to advance your career in other organizations. You are currently negotiating a new contract and rumors that you are switching jobs fast spreading in your company.

What should you do?

a.  You decide that since the rumor is already out, you update every one of your ongoing negotiations in the new company. You do this as it may even push your current directors to give you a promotion in the current company.

b.  Since nothing has been decided yet and it is still a rumor you maintain your silence on the issue until you give notice.

c.  Since you will probably leave and the rumor is already out, you invest less and less in your current position and invest more time in getting the new position.

d.  Since the rumor is out, you address your manager's doubts by updating him of your intentions of leaving and keep working normally since you are still an employee.

## 6. Scenario

The company you work for is having financial problems. You have come up with an innovative way to get more clients. The downside is the company will have to give up a loyal but less profitable client due to a conflict of interest. A few people on the marketing team agree, but your manager has a different opinion as he thinks the move is too risky.

What should you do?

a.  You withdraw your proposition as you trust your managers judgement and believe there is no reason to go against his judgement.

b.  You present a document that details the benefits your proposition will bring to the organization. But support his decision if he insists on it.

c.  You implement the idea despite your managers resistance as you have a lot of faith in the proposition. You trust your gut and implement the idea behind your manager's back for the companies benefit.

d.  You confront your manager and insist the idea is the best way out. You believe you are right you take the support of the marketing team and push your manager until he is convinced you are right.

## 7. Scenario

You are being undermined by a co-worker that has a junior position to you and has not been working there as long as you have. He is however considered a fast learner and is more educated than you. You get information from someone that the co-worker is interested in taking over your some of your roles.

What should you do?

a. Wait to see how it turns out as all this is hearsay and you consider it rumors.

b. You call the co-worker and talk to them, letting them know that cooperation is essential in any organization and you have something to learn form each other. You say that you will take more serious action if he refuses to understand.

c. You treat the matter with seriousness taking no chances. Your report your co-worker to your supervisor and advise him to replace the co-worker.

d. Since you don't want to turn the matter into a big issue, you seek the help of a third party in telling your co-worker that their behavior cannot be tolerated.

## 8. Scenario

You are the manager of a department where two members are long overdue to participate in a professional training course. The training manager lets you know that she has opted for individuals from a different department for the training.

You do not have a good relationship with the training department.

What should you do?

a. You reject the training manager's decision with a furious email demanding she re-opens the training as your employee's performance will be affected by their lack of training. You cc the email to the director.

b. You wait for the next training since your relationship with the training manager is already very poor.

c. You contact the manager of the other department and request a slot for one of your employees in the two slots he has been given.

d. You talk to the training manager to understand the reasons for her decision. You explain the importance of the training to your department and why it is necessary that your employee take it.

## 9. Scenario

Your employee has shown significant decline in sales in the past month. Although this decline has been happening for a while, it has significantly increased in the past two weeks. In addition, the employee has been coming to work late and seems frustration in her work. Since she is a popular employee who has been working at the company for 2 years, her behavior is influencing the work atmosphere.

What should you do?

a. Explain to her that her behavior is not just affecting not only her performance, her but the entire office. You express your intentions to help her through whatever she's going through on condition she improves her attitude.

b. Since she is a popular employee you feel it necessary to replace her temporarily to prevent a decline in office performance. You assign her back office tasks and assure her she will have her role back if her performance improves.

c. You schedule a staff meeting to discus the negative attitude you in the office. You point out the problematic employee and talk about how she is affecting the office atmosphere hoping she will change.

d. You let it blow over. Since she has consistently proved to be a good employee you feel no need to reprimand her. Part of your job is to accommodate employees when they face challenging situations.

## 10. Scenario

You are assigned a joint project with a co-worker who has been working in the department longer than you have. He does not put in much effort as he lacks the aspiration to develop professionally.

What should you do?

a. You accept the situation as it is and share the workload to the best of your ability. You leave the rest up to him.

b. You are concerned that poor quality work will effect your reputation and the company's reputation negatively and decide to put in extra hours to complete personally the project in the best way you can.

c. You contact your manger to report the situation as you cannot tolerate this attitude. You request the co-worker be replaced for the project.

d. You talk to the co-worker and negotiate that the work be distributed fairly between the two of you. You however consider the fact that you might have to put in extra effort to complete the project.

## 11. Scenario

You work as a consultant in an audit firm with five coworkers in your team reporting to a team manager who reports to a department manager.

Matt, a co-worker you share an office with, requires your advice on a report he is about to present the weekly team meeting. Your team manager leads the meetings but the department manager is present most of the time.

Although the part of the report Matt shows you looks fine, you observe missing conclusions of numerical analysis of a different section of the report. This does not meet the required standards of your departmental supervisor.
Matt looks confident about the part of the report and does

not seem interested in your opinion.
What should you do?

a.  There is not much you can do if he is not interested in your opinion. You let it go and let him face the consequences of presenting an incomplete report.

b.  Notify the management if he is not keen on listening to you. Talk to your manager and let him explain to Matt why the changes are necessary.

c.  Put in the necessary effort to make him listen. This may be a little uncomfortable, but you explain the reasons behind your criticism hoping Matt will understand.

d.  Try to educate him by showing him proper reports and company policy.

## 12. Scenario

You are working as a management trainee in a leisure company and are placed at a busy leisure club in the city center. You get a call from head office that a small leisure club has an abnormally large number of staff on off due to sickness today. Head office requests you spend time at that leisure club as the manager is off and his deputy is on holiday.

However, you have a pile of paperwork and several meetings with your team at your club.

What should you do?

a.  Explain your situation and inquire from the head office contact how you are supposed to prioritize your day.

b.  Suggest that you are given 30 minutes to reschedule your day and promise to give them a response after half an hour.

c.  Since you are busy suggest that they call other nearby clubs to find a manager who might be able to step in to help the understaffed club.

d.  Agree to spend time at the understaffed club but take your paperwork with you.

## 13. Scenario

You have been a graduate trainee with the government for close to six months. You joined the program with 3 trainees that you have been working with closely on several projects. You notice one of your colleagues has not been usual for a while.

You also over-hear your manager say she was not impressed by his contribution during a customer meeting. You and this colleague are supposed to deliver jointly work for a customer the following week.   You think he will not be able to deliver successfully.

What should you do?

a.  Take him for coffee and ask him how he is doing and express your concern that you are worried he has not been himself lately.

b.  Take him aside and explain to him that you can tell he is not functioning to his level best and offer to take up majority of the work on the following weeks project.

c.  Monitor him closely for a while, and intentionally find ways to work with him more closely.

d.  Approach your manager and let him know that you overheard him talk about your colleague. Let him know that you also think there are some problems.

## 14. Scenario

You hold a position as a graduate trainee position at a global bank branch. You have been requested by your manager to recommend options that will increase opportunities for business development within the branch. Several initiatives have been put in place to offer solutions for small businesses with little success. The team has been trained on the solutions and other branches have had success marketing them in their areas. The team in your branch is responsible for selling these packages with individual targets in place.

What should you do?

a. Talk to colleagues in branches that have been more successful and ask them what they are doing to be successful in their efforts to sale these packages.

b. Run another short training about the packages to the branch members responsible for selling them to customers.

c. Suggest that you come up with a free networking event for local businesses one evening at a nearby hotel.

d. Suggest you can call several local businesses to discuss the offer and try to close some sales personally.

## 15. Scenario

You noticed there is a lot of useful research conducted for clients while working as a graduate trainee for a consulting firm. You can see that clients and colleagues would benefit from this but there is no clear method to disseminate it. You discuss it with the manager and suggest ways to make the practice even better.

What should you do?

a.  Propose that you have a webinar every 90 days where key players in the company share findings from their research with others.

b.  Suggest a two-day internal conference every year that focusses on sharing research findings among employees.

c.  Suggest an area is created on the company internal network where employees are encouraged to share what they discover from their research.

d.  Suggest the company sets up a research forum with the purpose of ensuring the research findings are shared in the company with departmental representatives from all departments.


## 16. Scenario

You work as a trainee in a large bank. An upset client calls while you are working in the customer service department. He claims he has not received a refund on some fees he was charged in error.

He claims one of your colleagues promised the money would be in his account today but has not yet arrived. He is getting upset and raising his voice.

What should you say?

a.  "If you give me your account details, I will do all I can to investigate what happened."

b.  "Let me talk to the colleague you mentioned to get to the bottom of this. Please hold on a couple of minutes I will talk to him and get back to you."

c.  "I understand that you are upset but please calm down so that I can help you."

d.  "I believe there is a good reason for this. Give your account details so I can investigate."

## 17. Scenario

You are working in an electronics company as a trainee and are part of an international project looking at new marketing opportunities. You find it difficult to understand what a colleague is saying during a conference call. She is also a graduate trainee and during your interactions on other calls you have got on well. She has a strong accent and speaks very quickly when she is nervous. You are in the meeting room with several colleagues and the project lead. You can see that your colleagues are also having a difficult time understanding her.

What should you do?

    a. When she is no longer speaking, send her a private message explaining to her that she should slow down a little as several people are finding it difficult to understand her.

    b. Discuss your concerns after the call to other team members and suggest you compare notes to ensure you are on the same page.

    c. Mention your concerns to the project lead after the call and offer to talk to your colleague since you have a working relationship.

    d. Call your colleague after the call and ask how she finds the project. Politely mention that you find it difficult to understand what she says at times and suggest that slowing down would help.

## 18. Scenario

You submitted a paper to an upcoming professional global conference. You have attended the conference before and have met people from your industry and universities around the world. The paper has a summary of a research you conducted and believe it will be helpful. You learned that the paper has been accepted and you have been asked by your manager to find a way to present the paper that will make the biggest impact. You have limited time for your presentation.

How do you respond?

a.  Say you will employ the use of graphics and images to draw out key messages.

b.  Say you will create a presentation that reflects the research with similar section headers.

c.  Ask the manager what they think would be the best approach from their experience.

d.  Say that you will take time introducing the research approach but take most of the time talking about your findings and conclusions.

## 19. Scenario

You operate a 10-person group. You have professional and cooperative workers. However, you have recently found that they are taking longer breaks and work generally has been declining.  You are pleased that the workplace has a nice environment, but are concerned with the trend.

How should you respond?

a.  Announce that any employee wanting to take a break must first ask you about that.

b.  Announce that only one worker should have a coffee break at any specified moment.

c.  Speak to the staff regarding the situation and ask for cooperation.

d.  Warn team members with the deadlines and suggest there will be consequences.

## 20. Scenario

You feel some changes are needed after reading a study prepared by one of your team. When discussing the study with her, she disagrees with several of your statements and feels it is a strong report as is. What are you going to do?

    a.  Explain why your opinion more thoroughly.

    b.  Let her realize that your choices are final, but display empathy to her effort.

    c.  Tell her it is her job, and you value her view. Your feedback will support her, and she will be able to approve or deny it.

    d.  Invite her to discuss and clarify your remarks.

## 21. Scenario

You are asked to prepare a presentation for your staff, with the help of your co-worker, Daniel.  Your boss will make the presentation to the board of directors for approval. Daniel manages the data collection department. He is tasked with collecting data while you convert the data into PowerPoint slides. Daniel has gathered data from a paper that was incorrect - this has led you to create 30 misleading slides.

On the day you have the briefing, the supervisor counts on you to have everything ready with a lot more to do.

What is the best way to respond?

    a.  Describe to the boss how Daniel gathered the data and why it took a long time. Ask Daniel if he can fix the error he made- much of it was his own.

    b.  Let the boss know that you and Daniel got the data incorrect while putting together the presentation. Modify the introduction slides.

    c.  Do not call attention to this error. Give him handwritten notes during class with corrections to use while presenting.

    d.  Do not annoy the boss about this anymore. You can notify Daniel right away about changing the faulty slides.

## 22. Scenario

Bob is new to the office staff. Your superior, Dany, has asked you to teach Bob the computer system due to your experience. It is a relatively simple system, however, Bob is finding it difficult to understand. What should you do?

a. Tell him it should be easy for everyone to understand and he needs to learn it quickly.

b. Allow Anna, who has more experience than you, to conduct the lesson. Return to your other activities for the rest of the day.

c. Tell Bob to do it later. You become irritable and have to complete other tasks.

d. Discuss with Bob the issues he is having with the system. Start a new training session at a much simpler level.

## 23. Scenario

A client calls and criticizes you for not delivering a product by the deadline. You lookup the order and see the delivery is late due to a shortage.

What should you tell the client?

a. "I apologize; your order is delayed due to a shortage. Would you like me call when it is dispatched? "

b. "I am afraid we seem to be out of stock at the moment, but I'm certain your package will be delivered soon."

c. "The shipment has not yet been shipped; you are correct. We are out of stock right now, but I cannot do anything about that."

d. "I am afraid; this commodity seems to be out of stock now. For a while, you'll have to be careful."

## 24. Scenario

The store has just received a new brand of cell phone. Before marketing this new phone, which of the following is the most critical as a sales representative?

    a.  Ensure the new phone is displayed appropriately in the store.

    b.  Estimate the new product's impact on the market.

    c.  Review how competitors portray the new phone.

    d.  Test the commodity yourself and get acquainted with it.

## 25. Scenario

You work in department that shares office space with your colleagues. Everyone in your department is given a new computer system and you are left out.

What should you do?

    a. Consider this as a small mistake and talk to the head of department.

    b.  Confront the head of department and ask him to explain why you are being treated unfairly.

    c.  Take a new computer from a colleague.

    d.  Make a complaint with the HR department.

## 26. Scenario

You notice company property has been going missing for some time now. You noticed a colleague putting small things from the office in her handbag several times and suspect she is responsible.

What should you do?

a.  Find ways to get more evidence or catch her in the act.

b.  Face your colleague and ask her about what you have noticed then inform your manager of your suspicion.

c.  Raise the issue in a meeting and mention that you suspect your colleague.

d.  Don't do anything. Your colleague will be caught if she is guilty.


## 27. Scenario

After a busy day at work, you send an email with confidential information to a client by mistake.

What should you do?

a.  Leave the office and handle the matter the following day.

b.  Overlook the mistake, re-send the email to the correct address.

c.  Immediately contact the wrong recipient via phone or email to explain the mistake. Then send the email to the right person.

d.  Explain to your manager what happened and let them handle the matter.

## 28. Scenario

A patient suffering from a complex medical condition dies after a long period of treatment. Although there is enough evidence to fill a death certificate, your consultant is keen on taking a postmortem to investigate the death. The family consents to his request. However, the family speaks to you and claims they were coerced into making the decision and not happy.

What should you do?

    a.  Send the family back to the consultant and ask him to speak to them again.

    b.  Talk to your consultants and find out his reasons for the postmortem.

    c.  Request another senior colleague to meet with the family and discuss their concerns.

    d.  Personally, talk to the family about their concerns.

## 29. Scenario

Which action should be avoided when listening to an upset customer describing a problem?

    a.  Listen carefully to the customer describing the problem.

    b.  Politely requesting the customer to calm down that you can offer your assistance.

    c.  Directing the customer to your supervisor.

    d.  Putting effort on focusing the customer to their original need.

## 30. Scenario

You walk into the washroom and find a colleague crying.

What should you do?

    a.  Walk out and give them peace.

    b.  Find the manager and leave the situation to them.

    c.  Ask whether they are fine and if there is anything you can do to help.

    d.  Give them a hug at tell them everything will be okay.

## 31. Scenario

During your morning brief, the Infection Control instructs that all staff must roll up their sleeves when having clinical interactions with patients. During your shift, your colleague has her sleeves down.

What should you do?

    a.  Tell Infection Control that your colleague is not complying with their policy.

    b.  Speak directly to your colleague about your observation.

    c.  Raise your observation with to the nurse in charge of the ward.

    d.  Do not say anything immediately but monitor the situation over the course of the next few days.

## 32. Scenario

A patient with end-stage respiratory failure that requires continuous oxygen therapy informs you that he knows he is dying and wants to die at home. He has not talked about this to anyone as he thinks it will upset his family and the nurses taking care of him.

What would you do?

    a.  Tell him that he needs to stay in hospital while on oxygen.

    b.  Tell him that the team will take account of his wishes.

    c.  Discuss with his family his wish to die at home.

    d.  Discuss his home circumstances with his General Practitioner.

## 33. Scenario

A customer has been browsing in your department for ten minutes and seems progressively more and more disappointed. He comes toward you and asks if you have a specific manuscript that he is searching for, and after checking your computer, you need to advise him that it is 'unavailable'.

What should you do?

    a.  Apologize for the product not being available and recommend that he instead try to buy it online.

    b.  Place and order for customer and make sure they understand the delivery time. When it arrives, take the responsibility of calling immediately.

    c.  Provide the product information to the customer so they can order somewhere else.

    d.  Recommend other stores nearby.

## 34. Scenario

While communicating with your juniors and superiors, you realize you are distracted and several things are hindering you from staying actively engaged in the conversation.

How would you address this issue?

    a.  Start practicing yoga and wellness meditation.
    b.  Be keen and attentive while communicating.
    c.  Listen attentively without thinking.
    d.  Do not judge.

## 35. Scenario

You and your team encounter new challenges in a certain project. You realize the need to rally the team behind the difficult time.

How should you achieve this?

    a.  Show the team that you value their input.
    b.  Be harsh to the team members.
    c.  Assert your authority as a supervisor.
    d.  Dictate what needs to be done during hard times.

## 36. Scenario

You have been assigned a new type of project.  None of you are qualified to undertake the project.

How should you handle this situation?

    a.  Let the team know the deadlines to the set objectives.
    b.  Keep the information to yourself.
    c.  Call a meeting and strategize.
    d.  Use the internet to learn more.

## 37. Scenario

Prospective clients are very reluctant to sign up as customers. You need to convert and make sales because your supervisor is mounting pressure on you to produce.

How would you address this situation?

   a.  Carefully explain the product benefits to the prospective customers.

   b.  Switch to hard-sell sales techniques.

   c.  Ignore their objections.

   d.  Find prospects that are easier.

## 38. Scenario

After realizing losses for some time now, your supervisor blames you and your team. However, you know for sure that it was the supervisor who is responsible for the loss.

How should you handle the situation?

   a.  Blame the loss on the supervisor.

   b.  Take up this matter to higher authority.

   c.  Explain to the team that you are being blamed and strategize.

   d.  Deny the blame.

## 39. Scenario

You overhear discussions during coffee break about your planned termination. However, you feel that you are being wrongfully accused.

How would you react in such a situation?

   a.  Explain your side of the story.

   b.  Accuse other employees.

   c.  Blame the company.

   d.  Accept defeat and go home.

## 40. Scenario

You are required to collaborate with a coworker who is tough to please. For the success of the project, both of you need to work together.

What is the first step dealing with this situation?

    a.  Stay calm and try to understand their point of view.

    b.  Demean them and disregard their input.

    c.  Report to your supervisor that you can't work with them.

    d.  Ignore their unhelpful behavior.

# WCPT

# SENTENCE ORDER

**Instructions Questions 1 - 5:** The first sentence of a paragraph is given below, followed by additional sentences in the paragraph, listed in no particular order.  Order the sentences to create the best paragraph.  Make sure the paragraph is properly organized and grammatically correct.

**1. Peyton Manning is one of the most recognizable and respected football players in the history of the game.**

    A. After graduating, he played quarterback for the Indianapolis Colts for 14 years before he moved to Denver to lead the Broncos in 2012.

    B. Over the course of his years on the gridiron, he has earned many honors, including being named the NFL Player of the Decade for the years between 2000-2010.

    C. His other honors include being named the Most Valuable Player in the NFL in 2009 and being selected to 12 Pro Bowl teams.

    D. He first appeared on the national football radar as

the quarterback for the Volunteers of the University of Tennessee, where he helped lead the team to an SEC Championship in 1997.

E. During his time with the Colts, he was the MVP of Superbowl XLI when the Colt defeated the Chicago Bears in 2007.

**2. Roller coasters have been popular amusements for over 100 years.**

A. A few years later in 2003, Top Thrill Dragster was built to the height of 420 feet which is a long way from the small hills riders enjoyed 120 years before.

B. The first American roller coaster opened in 1884 at Coney Island.

C. Since that first ride was created, engineers have competed to design and build taller and faster coasters, like the first Giga-coaster, Millennium Force, which has a 310-foot hill and was built in 2000.

D. It is only a matter of time before roller coaster engineers create something bigger and taller to bring more fun to thrill seekers all over the world.

E. This early coaster was 600 feet long and operated with a switchback system where riders went one direction and then were sent back the way that they came.

**3. Learning to be a better baseball or softball player is not difficult to do.**

A. Another way to improve your game is to learn how to be an aggressive  base-runner who can cause defensive mistakes to happen.

B. There are three simple ways to improve your time on the field.

C. All three of these tips require a baseball player to be disciplined and learn the game to be successful on the field.

D. Finally, good baseball players know how to tire out the defense, whether they force the pitcher to throw more pitches, work hard to steal bases, or build a reputation of being a player that the defense needs to watch

E. The first way to be a better players is learn how to bunt, because many young players, as well as veteran players, have difficulty getting the ball and making an out.

## 4. Ultra-marathons are some of the most strenuous foot races on the planet.

A. Ultra-marathons can involve running a specific distance and some involve running for a specific amount of time.

B. One of the most popular ultra-marathons is the 100 kilometer race which is an event where runners can reach world records.

C. Runners  who want to go longer distances can run for 24 hours or they can choose to run on the 1000-mile races that require several days of running.

D. An ultra-marathon is a foot race where participants race for more than the 26.2 kilometers of the traditional marathon.

E. For runners who want the ultimate running experience, they can not only run on a mountainous trail, but through obstacle courses, and over challenging terrain; but these are only recommended for runners in outstanding condition.

## 5. As we look for ways to get energy from non-traditional sources, many people are turning to wind farms to provide energy for neighborhoods around the country.

A. The tall heights help wind turbines do their job.

B. Wind farms can vary in size; some have as few as five turbines and one has close to 5,000 individual turbines.

C. At those heights, stronger winds spin the blades faster which spins a motor that attaches to a generator to create more energy for surrounding homes and businesses.

D. Large wind turbines are between 230 and 265 feet tall, but when one blade is fully upright, they can reach over 400 feet in height.

E. Wind farm turbines need to be big and tall so they can create more electricity.

# READING

**Directions:** The following questions are based on several reading passages. A series of questions follow each passage. Read each passage carefully, and then answer the questions based on it. You may reread the passage as often as you wish. When you have finished answering the questions based on one passage, go right onto the next passage. Choose the best answer based on the information given and implied.

**Questions 1 and 2 refer to the following passage.**

**Women and Advertising**

Only in the last few generations have media messages been so widespread and so readily seen, heard, and read by so many people. Advertising is an important part of both selling and buying anything from soap to cereal to jeans. For whatever reason, more consumers are women than are men. Media message are subtle but powerful, and more attention has been paid lately to how these message affect women. Of all the products that women buy, makeup, clothes, and other stylistic or cosmetic products are among the most popular. This means that companies focus their advertising on women, promising them that their product will make her feel, look, or smell better than the next company's product will. This competition has resulted in advertising that is more and more ideal and less and less possible for everyday women. However, because women do look to these ideals and the products they represent as how they can potentially become, many women have developed unhealthy attitudes about themselves when they have failed to become those ideals.

In recent years, more companies have tried to change advertisements to be healthier for women. This includes featuring models of more sizes and addressing a huge outcry against unfair tools such as airbrushing and photo editing. There is debate about what the right balance between real and ideal is, because fashion is also considered art and some changes are made to purposefully elevate fashionable products and signify that they are creative, innovative, and the work of individual people. Artists want their freedom protected as much as women do, and advertising agencies are often caught in the middle.

Some claim that the companies who make these changes are not doing enough. Many people worry that there are still not enough models of different sizes and different ethnicities. Some people claim that companies use this healthier type of advertisement not for the good of women, but because they would like to sell products to the women who are looking for these kinds of messages. This is also a hard balance to find: companies do need to make money, and women do need to feel respected.

While the focus of this change has been on women, advertising can also affect men, and this change will hopefully be a lesson on media for all consumers.

**1. The second paragraph states that advertising focuses on women**

    a. to shape what the ideal should be

    b. because women buy makeup

    c. because women are easily persuaded

    d. because of the types of products that women buy

**2. The author uses the phrase "for whatever reason" in this passage to**

>   a. keep the focus of the paragraph on media messages and not on the differences between men and women
>
>   b. show that the reason for this is unimportant
>
>   c. argue that it is stupid that more women are consumers than men
>
>   d. show that he or she is tired of talking about why media messages are important

**Question 3 refers to the following passage.**

**FDR, the Treaty of Versailles, and the Fourteen Points**

At the conclusion of World War I, those who had won the war and those who were forced to admit defeat welcomed the end of the war and expected that a peace treaty would be signed. The American president, Franklin D. Roosevelt, played an important part in proposing what the agreements should be and did so through his Fourteen Points.
World War I had begun in 1914 when an Austrian archduke was assassinated, leading to a domino effect that pulled the world's most powerful countries into war on a large scale. The war catalyzed the creation and use of deadly weapons that had not previously existed, resulting in a great loss of soldiers on both sides of the fighting. More than 9 million soldiers were killed.

The United States agreed to enter the war right before it ended, and many believed that its decision to become finally involved brought on the end of the war. FDR made it very clear that the U.S. was entering the war for moral reasons and had an agenda focused on world peace. The Fourteen Points were individual goals and ideas (focused on peace, free trade, open communication, and self reliance) that FDR wanted the power nations to strive for now that the war had concluded. He was optimistic and had many ideas about what could be accomplished through and during the post-war peace. However, FDR's fourteen points were poorly received when he presented them to the leaders of other world powers, many of whom wanted only to help their own countries and to punish the Germans for fuelling the war, and they fell by the wayside. World War II was imminent, for Germany lost everything.

Some historians believe that the other leaders who participated in the Treaty of Versailles weren't receptive to the Fourteen Points because World War I was fought almost entirely on European soil, and the United States lost much less than did the other powers. FDR was in a unique position to determine the fate of the war, but doing it on his own terms did not help accomplish his goals. This is only one historical example of how the United State has tried to use its power as an important country, but found itself limited because of geological or ideological factors.

**3. The main idea of this passage is that**

> a. World War I was unfair because no fighting took place in America

> b. World War II happened because of the Treaty of Versailles

> c. the power the United States has to help other countries also prevents it from helping other countries

> d. Franklin D. Roosevelt was one of the United States' smartest presidents.

# CORRECTING SENTENCES

## Abuse of Science: The Atom Bomb

### Questions 4 - 7 refer to the following passage

The cost of the two World Wars – not to mention the lives lost – could have easily paid for the entire energy consumption of the nations which waged them. [1] Even today, world powers are spending hundreds of billions of dollars sponsoring wars in a bid to control oil-rich areas. [2] Spending such astronomic sums on peaceful, environment friendly sources of energy would certainly produce results that would limit the energy needs of the planet as a whole. [3] Not to mention, resolving the conflicts between warring nations. [4]

For instance the atom bomb was developed during the Second World War by the recommendations of the great Albert Einstein - who is accepted as the father of modern physics; in fear of the Germans developing it and using on the Allies. [5]  No matter what, the technology behind the atom bomb essentially had the power to resolve the war. [6] Using it to produce energy for power was an option wide open to be explored by scientists. [7] Today, as many as forty countries including countries like Egypt, harness nuclear energy as a dominant source of power alongside mainstream carbon sources. [8]

The two atom bombs dropped at Hiroshima and Nagasaki, as the consequence of the tragedy at Pearl Harbor, left catastrophic legacies to the generations that followed. [9] The generations that followed still have not recovered from the genetic disorders. [10]  Almost seven decades passing later, abnormal births and birth defects continue to occur. [11]

**4. Which sentence from the passage is an example of a sentence fragment?**

    a. 3

    b. 4

    c. 5

    d. 6

## 5. Which of the following changes would focus attention on the main idea of the second paragraph?

a. Yet, the technology behind the atom bomb essentially had the power of resolving the war itself which scientists like him failed to convey.

b. As a result of that, the technology behind the atom bomb essentially had the power of resolving the war itself which scientists like him failed to convey.

c. With respect to that, the technology behind the atom bomb essentially had the power of resolving the war itself which scientists like him failed to convey.

d. Additionally, the technology behind the atom bomb essentially had the power of resolving the war itself which scientists like him failed to convey.

## 6. Which of the following changes are needed in sentence 5?

a. For instance the atom bomb was developed during the Second World War by the recommendations of the great Albert Einstein - who is accepted as the father of modern physics - in fear of the Germans developing it and using on the Allies.

b. For instance, the atom bomb was developed during the Second World War by the recommendations of the great Albert Einstein - who is accepted as the father of modern physics - in fear of the Germans developing it and using on the Allies.

c. For instance, the atom bomb was developed during the Second World War by the recommendations of the great Albert Einstein; who is accepted as the father of modern physics - in fear of the Germans developing it and using on the Allies.

d. For instance, the atom bomb was developed during the Second World War by the recommendations of the great Albert Einstein; who is accepted as the father of modern physics, in fear of the Germans developing it and using on the Allies.

**7. Which of the following sentences, if inserted before sentence 7, would best illustrate the main idea of the passage?**

a. The name of the technology is widely referred to in current science books published worldwide as nuclear fission.

b. This technology is, however, misused by many irresponsible states in the world today.

c. Nuclear fission that is used in the fuelling of the bomb, has the capacity to produce electrical energy which has turned out to be a major alternative later in the Twentieth Century.

d. Nuclear fission, which is the main technology behind the development of the atom bomb can also be used to produce gamma rays which has many applications in medical science.


# Leg Surgery


**Questions 8 - 11 refer to the following passage**

The main reason many young women opt for surgery, despite the pain, inconvenience and cost, is the height discrimination in an increasingly competitive job market. [1] Almost all firms put certain height criteria for the candidates who apply. [2] For example, for an air stewardess position, women must be no more than 163 cm tall; whereas for jobs in foreign affairs, Chinese diplomats are required to match their foreign counterparts. [3] Height concerns also effect routine citizenship privileges such as driving licenses, which require a height of at least 157 cm to be eligible for taking the test in some places. [4]

The urge to undergo surgery is becoming increasingly popular among Chinese males as well. [5] "It offers me a 10 cm increase in my height, which can dramatically change my future," says Jing Yong, an interpreter working in Hong Kong. [6] "This will allow me better opportunities in the competitive job market here," adds the young multilingual who couldn't make it to the foreign ministry for being below 168 cm. [7]

Even parents approve of the idea, being fully aware of all the complexity and they are willing to finance such a labyrinth surgery. [8] "It's something that will give her confidence and achieve her goals in life. [9] Her height used to bother her tremendously, now this can change that," comments Swee Jing's father by her bedside as she is recovering from the eighteen-months process that involves elongating her tibia and fibula by placing two rods that will stimulate the extra growth of the bones. [10] They too are hopeful about the possibilities the surgery would affect the life of their daughter. [11]

**8. Which sentence in the second paragraph is least relevant to the main idea of the first paragraph?**

   a. 2

   b. 3

   c. 4

   d. 5

**9. Which sentence is not consistent with the author's purpose?**

   a. 3

   b. 6

   c. 9

   d. 12

**10. Which of the following sentences, if inserted after sentence 7, would best illustrate the main idea of the passage?**

a. This is the main reason I am willing to undergo this surgery

b. This artificial way of gaining height is turning out to be a new trend among the new generation in height conscious China.

c. Height is a very big problem for Chinese people, particularly for those who wish to go abroad and carry the flag of China there.

d. Young people like Yong will have to spend the rest of their lives with a fake pair of legs though.

**11. Which of the following changes are needed in sentence 8?**

a. Even parents approve of the idea, being fully aware of all the sophistications and they are willing to finance such a labyrinth surgery.

b. Even parents approve of the idea, being fully aware of all the complications and they are willing to finance such a sophisticated surgery.

c. Even parents approve of the idea, being fully aware of all the complexity and they are willing to finance such a sophisticated surgery.

d. Even parents approve of the idea, being fully aware of all the complexity and they are willing to finance such a sophisticated surgery.

## My Friend Luke

**Questions 12 - 15 refer to the following passage**

My forty-year old friend Luke is possibly the sweetest, shyest person enjoying his life on the entire Earth. [1] He is somewhat short, skinny and upright; has a thin moustache and a thinner trace of hair covering his head. [2] And since he has problems seeing distant things, he wears glasses that are small, thick and frameless; the round coffee-brown colored glasses give him a cool appearance uniquely suited to his personality. [3] Which I doubt belongs to any other person. [4]

There are traits in him seldom found in others. [5] While in a crowd, he walks sideways so as not to trouble others. [6] Instead of requesting a space to move ahead, he glides past to one side of the person blocking in his way. [7] If the gap turns out to be so narrow that it does not permit his bony frame to pass, he waits patiently for the person to move out of the way. [8] He is panicked by street dogs and neighbors' cats and to avoid them, he crosses to the other side of the street every now and then. [9]

Luke never speaks, as he thinks speaking is a waste of energy; something he is vehemently dedicated to saving. [10]  Whenever he does, in order not to interrupt anybody, he speaks with a very soft, low tone – in a way no one ever notices him speaking in the first place. [11] Quite ironically, when he gets a rare chance to speak, he never succeeds in speaking more than two words before being interrupted by others. [12]

**12. What sentence from the passage is an example of a sentence fragment?**

    a. 4

    b. 5

    c. 6

    d. 7

**13. Which sentence in the second paragraph is least relevant to the main idea of the second paragraph?**

    a. 6

    b. 7

    c. 8

    d. 9

**14. Which of the following sentences should be modified to reduce redundancy?**

    a. 2

    b. 3

    c. 4

    d. 5

**15. Which of the following sentences, if inserted before sentence 1, would best illustrate the main idea of the passage?**

    a. But that does not bother him; rather he always seems to be happy in being able to utter those two words.

    b. Interestingly, he never insists in speaking with people more eloquently.

    c. What is more ironic, he never worked on his social skills and diction to be more communicative.

    d. As a result, Luke feels like hitting those interrupting him in their face.

## Of Ease and Discipline

**Questions 16 - 19 refer to the following passage**

Looking at his watch, Ray thought it was time for a break. [1] So, he let the kids wrap their things up and head out of the classroom. [2] They seemed to like the idea of an extra five minutes before they would start with the boring recitation, turning page after page as one of them stood and read through the old Shakespearean dialect. [3] Some were interested in chatting with him as they approached him with the usual curiosity about a new teacher joining their class. [4] What they didn't know was he was their new music teacher just replacing the dull Mr. Drodsky who happened to be an 'expert' in American Literature with his dreadful Eastern European accent. [5] But for a day only. [6]

They were excited about the rhetoric that they finally have

been spared of Mr. Drodsky's shrieking inquiries of "Aa you wiss me, chilsren?" [7]  But as they came to know him closely, they were disappointed he would only occupy Mr. Drodsky's position for  two weeks. [8]  Mr. Drodsky was ill and would be away for the next fifteen days. [9] They seemed to like the news, but were also reluctant to be happy about it. [10] Nevertheless, they were happy about the substitution today and the arrival of their new music teacher. [11] The school would return to their jolly old days with regular music lessons and the parties. [12]
With ring of the bell, all the boys and girls started filling their seats as Ray continued chatting with the ones who had asked him about himself. [13] In a moment all the students – out of their old habits – were ready with their books open, waiting for the teacher to dictate who was in queue to read. [14] Ray was somewhat perplexed as he found this obedience unusual, especially in this century. [15] Coming from a public school in New Jersey, Ray had never seen students 'tamed' to such narrow, desperate discipline in his six years of experience as a music teacher. [16]

**16. What sentence from the passage is an example of a sentence fragment?**

    a. 3

    b. 4

    c. 5

    d. 6

**17. Which sentence is not consistent with the author's purpose?**

    a. 6

    b. 7

    c. 9

    d. 10

**18. Which of the following changes are needed in sentence 16?**

a. Coming from a public school in New Jersey, Ray had never seen students 'tamed' to such narrow, disparate discipline in his six years of experience as a music teacher.

b. Coming from a public school in New Jersey, Ray had never seen students 'tanned' to such narrow, disparate discipline in his six years of experience as a music teacher.

c. Coming from a public school in New Jersey, Ray had never seen students 'turned' to such narrow, desperate discipline in his six years of experience as a music teacher.

d. No change.

**19. Which of the following sentences contains non-standard usage?**

a. 4

b. 5

c. 6

d. 7

# Spiderman

**Question 20 refers to the following passage**

Spiders have always fascinated Johnson. [1] Ever since his childhood visit to his grandfather's farm in Vancouver where he first saw them in a large web that almost covered the gate of the granary warehouse, he looked for spiders everywhere he visited. [2] He would search for spider webs even in the high rise apartments such as the one he lives in now. [3] He would find them there too. [4] Hanging between two walls near one corner of the store room, a magnificent piece of art left half woven and still being worked on. [5]

It is not the life of the spiders itself that attracted Johnson, rather their art. [6] He likes their delicate webs. [7] The amazing shape and sizes of the webs. [8] The symmetry, the balance, the intricate design and the detailed network fascinates him. [9] He wanders how they manage to create something unique like this with such a little brain that they have. [10] That is why he likes to catch them in action, while they are weaving. [11]

When he opened the store room this week, he saw the huge web in the left corner touching the roof. [12] That has been there for almost six months now and it lay there as it were last month. [13] No strands added. [14] It took on a grayish shade from the dust it gathered over the weeks, making it obvious that Binny has stopped working on it. [15] Hanging here and there in the web are some dry mosquitoes that were spared by the monster that owns the trap. [16]

In the far left, on the wall adjacent to the door, Johnson is trying to build a web out of string and glue -without much success! [17] "Incredible, you little genius!" Johnson murmurs to himself. [18]

**20. What sentence from the passage is an example of a sentence fragment?**

    a. 2

    b. 3

    c. 4

    d. 5

# VOCABULARY

**1. Choose the adjective that means shocking, terrible or wicked.**

    a. Pleasantries

    b. Heinous

    c. Shrewd

    d. Provencal

**2. Choose the noun that means a person of thing that tells or announces the coming of someone or something.**

- a. Harbinger
- b. Evasion
- c. Bleak
- d. Craven

**3. Choose a word that means the same as the underlined word.**

**He wasn't especially generous.  All the servings were very <u>judicious</u>.**

- a. Abundant
- b. Careful
- c. Sparing
- d. Careless

**4. Because of the growing use of _________ as a fuel, corn production has greatly increased.**

- a. Alcohol
- b. Ethanol
- c. Natural gas
- d. Oil

**5. In heavily industrialized areas, the pollution of the air causes many to develop _________ diseases.**

- a. Respiratory
- b. Cardiac
- c. Alimentary
- d. Circulatory

**6. Choose the best definition of inherent.**

    a. To receive money in a will

    b. An essential part of

    c. To receive money from a will

    d. None of the above

**7. Choose the best vapid.**

    a. adj. tasteless or bland

    b. v. To inflict, as a revenge or punishment

    c. v. to convert into gas

    d. v. to go up in smoke

**8. Choose the best definition of waif.**

    a. n. a sick and hungry child

    b. n. an orphan staying in a foster home

    c. n. homeless child or stray

    d. n. a type of French bread eaten with cheese

**9. Choose the adjective that means similar or identical.**

    a. Soluble

    b. Assembly

    c. Conclave

    d. Homologous

**10. Choose a word with the same meaning as the underlined word.**

**We used that operating system 20 years ago, now it is <u>obsolete</u>.**

    a. Functional

    b. Disused

    c. Obese

    d. None of the Above

**11. Choose the word with the same meaning as the underlined word**

**His bad manners really <u>rankle</u> me.**

    a. Annoy

    b. Obsolete

    c. Enliven

    d. None of the above

**12. Because hydroelectric power is a __________ source of energy, its use is excellent for the environment.**

    a. Significant

    b. Disposable

    c. Renewable

    d. Reusable

**13. Choose the best definition of torpid.**

    a. Fast

    b. Rapid

    c. Sluggish

    d. Violent

**14.  Choose the best definition of gregarious.**

a. Sociable

b. Introverted

c. Large

d. Solitary

**15. Choose the best definition of mutation.**

a. v. To utter with a loud and vehement voice

b. n. change or alteration

c. n. An act or exercise of will

d. v. To cause to be one

**16. Choose the best definition of lithe.**

a. adj. small in size

b. adj. Artificial

c. adj. flexible or plaint

d. adj. fake

**17. Choose the best definition of resent.**

a. adj. To express displeasure or indignation

b. v. To cause to be one

c. adj. Clumsy

d. adj. strong feelings of love

**18. Choose and adjective that means irrelevant or not having substance or matter**

a. Immaterial

b. Prohibition

c. Prediction

d. Brokerage

**19. Choose and adjective that means perfect, no faults or errors.**

>  a. Impeccable
>
>  b. Formidable
>
>  c. Genteel
>
>  d. Disputation

**20. Choose the best definition of pudgy.**

>  a. v. to draw general inferences
>
>  b. Adj. fat, plump and overweight
>
>  c. n. permanence
>
>  d. adj. spoilt or bad condition

# English Grammar, Punctuation, Capitalization and Usage.

**1. Jessica's father was in the Navy, so she attended schools in <u>Newark; New Jersey, Key West; Florida, San Diego, California, and Fairbanks, Alaska.</u>**

>  a. Jessica's father was in the Navy, so she attended schools in Newark, New Jersey, Key    West, Florida, San Diego, California, and Fairbanks, Alaska.
>
>  b. Jessica's father was in the Navy, so she attended schools in: Newark, New Jersey, Key West, Florida, San Diego, California, and Fairbanks, Alaska.
>
>  c. Jessica's father was in the Navy, so she attended schools in Newark, New Jersey; Key West, Florida; San Diego, California; and Fairbanks, Alaska.
>
>  d. None of the choices are correct.

**2. George wrecked John's <u>car; that</u> was the end of their friendship.**

    a. George wrecked John's car that was the end of their friendship.

    b. George wrecked John's car. that was the end of their friendship.

    c. The sentence is correct.

    d. None of the choices are correct.

**3. The dress was not Gina's <u>favorite, however,</u> she wore it to the dance.**

    a.   The dress was not Gina's favorite; however, she wore it to the dance.

    b.   None of the choices are correct.

    c.   The dress was not Gina's favorite, however; she wore it to the dance.

    d.   The dress was not Gina's favorite however, she wore it to the dance.

**4. Chris showed his dedication to golf in many <u>ways; for</u> example, he watched all the tournaments on television.**

    a. Chris showed his dedication to golf in many ways, for example, he watched all the tournaments on television.

    b. The sentence is correct.

    c. Chris showed his dedication to golf in many ways, for example; he watched all the tournaments on television.

    d. Chris showed his dedication to golf in many ways for example he watched all the tournaments on television.

**5. There was scarcely <u>no food</u> in the pantry, because <u>not nobody</u> ate at home.**

    a. There was scarcely no food in the pantry, because nobody ate at home.

    b. There was scarcely any food in the pantry, because nobody ate at home.

    c. There was scarcely any food in the pantry, because not nobody ate at home.

    d. The sentence is correct.

**6. Choose the sentence with the correct grammar.**

    a. If Joe had told me the truth, I wouldn't have been so angry.
    b. If Joe would have told me the truth, I wouldn't have been so angry.
    c. I wouldn't have been so angry if Joe would have told the truth.
    d. If Joe would have telled me the truth, I wouldn't have been so angry.

**7. Michael <u>have lived</u> in that house for forty years, while I <u>has owned</u> this one for only six weeks.**

    a. Michael has lived in that house for forty years, while I has owned this one for only six weeks.

    b. Michael have lived in that house for forty years, while I have owned this one for only six weeks.

    c. None of the choices are correct.

    d. Michael has lived in that house for forty years, while I have owned this one for only six weeks.

**8. Until you <u>take</u> the overdue books to the library, you can't <u>take</u> any new ones home.**

    a.  Until you take the overdue books to the library, you can't take any new ones home

    b.  Until you take the overdue books to the library, you can't bring any new ones home.

    c.  Until you bring the overdue books to the library, you can't take any new ones home.

    d.  None of the choices are correct.

**9. If they had <u>gone</u> to the party, he would have <u>gone</u> too.**

    a. The sentence is correct.

    b. If they had went to the party, he would have gone too.

    c. If they had gone to the party, he would have went too.

    d. If they had went to the party, he would have went too.

**10. His doctor suggested that he eat <u>fewer</u> snacks and do <u>fewer</u> lounging on the couch.**

    a.  His doctor suggested that he eat less snacks and do fewer lounging on the couch.

    b.  His doctor suggested that he eat fewer snacks and do less lounging on the couch.

    c.  His doctor suggested that he eat less snacks and do less lounging on the couch.

    d. None of the choices are correct.

**11. Lee pronounced <u>it's</u> name incorrectly; <u>it's</u> an impatiens, not an impatience.**

    a. The sentence is correct.

    b. Lee pronounced its name incorrectly; its an *impatiens*, not an *impatience.*

    c. Lee pronounced it's name incorrectly; its an *impatiens*, not an *impatience.*

    d. Lee pronounced its name incorrectly; it's an *impatiens*, not an *impatience.*

**12. There <u>was, however</u> very little difference between the two.**

    a.  There was however, very little difference between the two.

    b.  None of the choices are correct.

    c.  There was; however, very little difference between the two.

    d.  There was, however, very little difference between the two.

**13. The Ford Motor Company was named for Henry Ford**

    a. which had founded the company.

    b. who founded the company.

    c. whose had founded the company.

    d. whom had founded the company.

**14.  Thomas Edison __________ after he invented the light bulb, television, motion pictures, and phonograph.**

    a. has always been known as the greatest inventor

    b. was always been known as the greatest inventor

    c. must have had been always known as the greatest inventor

    d. will had been known as the greatest inventor

**15.  The weatherman on Channel 6 said that this has been the _________.**

a.  most hottest summer on record.

b.  hottest summer on record.

c.  hotter summer on record.

d.  None of the above

**16.  Although Joe is tall for his age, his brother Elliot is _________ of the two.**

a. the tallest

b. more tallest

c. the tall

d. the taller

**17.  I can never remember how to use those two common words, "sell," meaning to trade a product for money, or _________ meaning an event where products are traded for less money than usual.**

a. sale-

b. "sale,"

c. "sale

d. "to sale,"

**18. His father is**

a.  a poet and novelist

b.  poet and novelist

c.  a poet and a novelist

d.  none of the above

**19. The class just finished reading , __________ a short story by Carl Stephenson about a plantation owner's battle with army ants.**

    a. -"Leinengen versus the Ants,"

    b. Leinengen versus the Ants,

    c. "Leinengen versus the Ants,"

    d. Leinengen versus the Ants

**20. After the car was fixed it __________ again.**

    a. ran good

    b. ran well

    c. would have run well

    d. ran more well

**21. "Where does the sun go during the __________ asked little Kathy.**

    a. night,"

    b. night?",

    c. night,?"

    d. night?"

**22. Vegetables are a <u>healthy</u> food; eating them can make you more <u>healthy</u>.**

    a. Vegetables are a healthy food; eating them can make you more healthful.

    b. Vegetables are a healthful food; eating them can make you more healthful.

    c. None of the choices are correct.

    d. Vegetables are a healthful food; eating them can make you more healthy.

**23. When James went <u>in</u> his room, he found that his clothes had been put <u>in</u> the closet.**

    a. When James went into his room, he found that his clothes had been put in the closet.

    b.  None of the choices are correct.

    c. When James went into his room, he found that his clothes had been put into the closet.

    d. When James went in his room, he found that his clothes had been put into the closet.

**24.  After you lay the books on the counter, you may lay down for a nap.**

    a. The sentence is correct.

    b. After you lie the books on the counter, you may lay down for a nap.

    c. After you lay the books on the counter, you may lie down for a nap.

    d. After you lay the books on the counter, you may lay down for a nap.

**25. Don <u>would never of thought</u> of that book, but you <u>could have reminded</u> him.**

    a.  Don would never have thought of that book, but you could have reminded him.

    b.  None of the choices are correct.

    c.  Don would never have thought of that book, but you could of  have reminded him.

    d.  Don would never of thought of that book, but you could of reminded him.

**26. Mrs. Foster <u>learned</u> me many things, but I was <u>taught</u> the most by Mr. Wallace.**

    a. Mrs. Foster taught me many things, but I learned the most from Mr. Wallace.

    b.  The sentence is correct.

    c. Mrs. Foster learned me many things, but I learned the most from Mr. Wallace.

    d. None of the choices are correct.

**27.  He did not have to <u>loose</u> the race; if only his shoes weren't so <u>loose</u>!**

    a. He did not have to loose the race; if only his shoes weren't so lose!

    b. He did not have to lose the race; if only his shoes weren't so loose!

    c. The sentence is correct.

    d. None of the choices are correct.

**28.  The attorney did not want to <u>prosecute</u> the defendant; his goal was to <u>prosecute</u> the guilty party.**

    a. None of the choices are correct.

    b. The attorney did not want to persecute the defendant; his goal was to persecute the guilty party.

    c. The attorney did not want to prosecute the defendant; his goal was to persecute the guilty party.

    d. The attorney did not want to persecute the defendant; his goal was to prosecute the guilty party.

**29. The speeches must <u>proceed</u> the election; the election cannot <u>proceed</u> without hearing from the candidates.**

a. The speeches must precede the election; the election cannot proceed without hearing from the candidates.

b. The speeches must precede the election; the election cannot precede without hearing from the candidates.

c. The speeches must proceed the election; the election cannot precede without hearing from the candidates.

d. The sentence is correct.

**30. My best friend said, "Always Count your Change."**

a. My best friend said, "always count your change."

b. The sentence is correct.

c. My best friend said, "Always count your change."

d. None of the choices are correct.

**31. The <u>Victorian Era</u> was in the <u>nineteenth century</u>.**

a. The sentence is correct.

b. The victorian era was in the nineteenth century.

c. The Victorian Era was in the Nineteenth century.

d. The Victorian era was in the Nineteenth century.

**32. I prefer <u>pepsi</u> to <u>Coke</u>.**

a. I prefer pepsi to coke.

b. The sentence is correct.

c. I prefer Pepsi to Coke.

d. None of the choices are correct.

**33. I always have <u>french fries</u> with my <u>coke</u>.**

    a. The sentence is correct.

    b. I always have french fries with my Coke.

    c. I always have French Fries with my Coke.

    d. None of the choices are correct.

**34. The <u>blue Jays</u> are my favorite team.**

    a. The blue jays are my favorite team.

    b. The sentence is correct.

    c. The Blue Jays are my favorite team.

    d. None of the choices are correct.

**35. The <u>Southwest</u> is the best part of the country.**

    a.  The sentence is correct.
    b.  The southwest is the best part of the country.
    c.  The southwest is the best part of the Country.
    d.  None of the choices are correct.

# ANSWER KEY

## SITUATIONAL JUDGEMENT

### 1. C

Going over your head is disrespectful of your authority. Even though the new idea will make their work easier, some employees are resistant to change. Inviting them for a discussion demonstrates that you are serious about the idea and that you are available for discussions in case of a problem.

Ignoring the mistake, choice A, to avoid conflict will send a signal that you are scared of conflict. Punishing the employee, choice B, will probably cause resentment.

### 2. C

As a professional, you need to rise above personal conflict, even if others are not. Giving a professional opinion and risk going into the bad books of one of your superiors demonstrates that you are ready to risk personal gratification for the team's success.

Refusing to pick a side, or picking a side based on politics, might be a safe option to choose to a short-cited individual. This will not serve the organizational and both the manager and supervisor will be able to read your weakness in decision making. It will be clear to them you cannot make a decision for the benefit of the company.

### 3. C

This scenario has shown us that the deputy director is not incompetent but is arrogant and disloyal. This course will only improve her academic qualification but will not address he arrogance and disloyalty. Talking to her will open up her mind to her weaknesses and give her a chance to reflect on them and correct. Informing the director will enable him find a solution to her weaknesses and find a way of helping her without compromising the company goals.

Approving her application without talking to her, (choice A) will only shift the problem from your department to the department she will be transferred to. Talking to the director without trying to address the issue first,(choice D), will not help her as she might lose the opportunity.

## 4. B
One should not allow their personal life to affect their professional life. To effectively cope with a volatile market, consult more experienced salespeople.

## 5. D
It is the responsibility of the employee to inform their manager of their intention to leave. This will help the manager in planning for the future. It will also give the manager a chance to address issues that might have caused you to look elsewhere for employment. It is also important to continue working normally as you are still an employee of the company you work for.

## 6. B
You need to make an effort to convince the manager by educating him on the benefits of the idea backed by evidence without arguing with him in the presence of his subordinates. You also have a duty and obligation to support whatever decision the manager makes even if you believe you have a better idea.

## 7. B
By selecting choice B you will show honesty and genuine interest in the issue at hand. This serves the purpose of educating your co-worker on the benefits of cooperation. It is fair to take more action if the co-worker chooses to ignore your advice.

## 8. D
Choice D is the most effective. This might even give you a chance to sort out your strained relationship.

## 9. A
By selecting choice A as a manager, you have decided to solve the problem in a proactive way. Addressing the problem by talking to the employee will assure her that you care. As an employee that has consistently performed well talking to her will enable the manager get a better understanding of

the problem she is facing and better help her.

Calling a staff meeting to address a personal problem, choice C, is a waste of time and a counter productive move. Publicly reprimanding a popular employee will only worsen the situation as she might feel offended. The employee might turn resentful and the hope that the behavior will improve might never come.

## 10. D
A joint project requires team work and team work requires communication and constant negotiation on what should be done and how it should be done. Negotiating and distributing the work fairly between the two of you will ensure he steps up and takes responsibility for his part of the project. However, because of the situation and poor performance will reflect badly on you as well, be prepared to put in some extra.

## 11. A
You have tried to help, and that is the best that you can do. Choice B, notifying the management seems excessive at this point.  Choice D, trying to educate him is using up your time and effort, and since he doesn't seem receptive, probably a waster of time.

## 12. A
As an employee you are supposed to be flexible and be ready to help when needed. As much the management trainee is held up by other responsibilities explaining the situation to head office might help as his meetings can be rescheduled and the deadlines on the paperwork extended.

## 13. A
Talking to him will let him know that people care about him. He might be able to open up and talk about the challenges he is facing. Venting might help him relax and focus on his work better.

Remember you aren't a counsellor but a friend and co-worker and this is a casual conversation.

## 14. A

Speaking to colleagues of other branches that have been successful is the best solution. Learning from the successful branches will save you wasted energy and time.  Other choices, such as choice C, a networking event, or choice D, calling customers personally are good second steps.

## 15. D

Choice D gives the company a continuous way of sharing research findings. Creating a research forum will give employees a chance to discuss all matters research as much as they want in the forum. Having people from different departments will mean they can be able to share ideas and expertise constantly.

## 16. A

By choosing choice A the client will be assured that their issue will be taken care of. This response makes no superficial promises and no blame is shifted to the bank or the other colleague.

## 17. D

Calling her after the call will enable you maximize on the good relationship you already have and she will probably be more receptive. Politely mentioning that you find it difficult to understand her will be helpful as she might not be aware that her accent affects, her communication and slowing down will be a good solution provided.  This choice does not escalate the situation as discussing with other team member (choice B) as well as the project lead (choice C).

## 18. C

The manager, from their experience, will have ideas on the best way to present the material with the greatest impact. Asking for his guidance will enable you tap into his experience and make an impactful presentation.

## 19. C

Your workers' self-discipline is lacking and is presently harming their performance. You understand your team's good qualities and want to protect it, but are still anxious about the potential of your team. Team members are friendly and have demonstrated particularly good success in the past, so appealing to their collaboration is most likely to produce results. This direct contact demonstrates the capacity to efficiently connect and control workers and to effectively use methods to improve efficiency. This approach aims to promote employee growth and development.

Introducing targets and pushing them may be a feasible tactic. It is a good form of rising efficiency. Nevertheless, this reaction often involves a punitive measure, which is too early to pursue.

## 20. D

Choice D will be the one that encourages a genuine debate. This answer gives you more details, and you can consider together with your employee in a clear exchange of views (decision making - taking staff input). This reply demonstrates that you value the viewpoint of your staff while respecting and retaining your own opinion. It is the safest option.  Different situations require   different approaches to authority - in some roles; you must be stern. In contrast, in others, an approach to instructional oversight is favored (as a guide). Choice D is the best option because it indicates that you care about your subordinates' input in the decision-making phase.

## 21. B

Selecting choice B, demonstrates responsibility and acceptance of the effects of one's actions. Daniel was more responsible than you for making the mistake. However, by sharing that responsibility with your teammate, you show that you are a team player (teamwork). Suppose you let your boss know that you have made a mistake. In that case, you are showing that you are responsible and have the integrity of admitting your mistakes – thus allowing your boss to be considerate of the possibility of being late for the deadline. When you and your team work together to add an amendment to the document organically, it allows you to perfect your submission on time.

Choice A may sound like the right solution because Daniel is responsible for the issue. However, you are not prepared to divide the guilt, so you are dropping all the burden on Daniel and not offering to work together on fixing the issue.

Besides, you can unintentionally harm his reputation with the boss by attacking Daniel behind his back— as he should be offered a chance to clarify.

## 22. A

It is the only approach when you search for the root of Bob's issues.  Understanding what he finds challenging, you are showing strong listening skills. You often demonstrate adaptability by adjusting the solution to the issue. By being supportive and providing answers, you are a team player to improve the understanding of your colleague.

It might be more beneficial to let another worker with more expertise take over. However, your boss has assigned you this assignment, and it is not your duty to assign it to anyone else. Most likely, the issue does not rely on the degree of expertise but the method of teaching. You do not demonstrate the adaptability of your method of teaching by letting Anna teach him.

## 23. C

This answer is clear and direct. Choice A starts by apologizing. The response given in this reply option adds an invitation to contact the customer, giving additional service and explaining operation and service guidance.
Choice C understands the customer's concern but has no constructive effort ("I cannot do anything"), giving the appearance you are not accountable for the issue.

## 24. D

This question assesses how you navigate the transition to marketing a new product (adaptability). The most important approach is to familiarize yourself with the product by checking it yourself (choice D). As a sales agent, you need to be comfortable when showing it to customers.

It is necessary to ensure that the product display is attractive and appropriate (choice A) but not critical. It is interesting to read the product's success (choice B), which may help with your sales, but not critical. It is important and may be useful, to see what competitors are doing, (choice C) but also not critical.

**25. A**

Choice A is the best response. If you have not been given the right tools and equipment to do your job, talking to your head of department or direct supervisor is the right move. It is the responsibility of your head of department to help ensure you have all it takes to do your job.

Jumping to conclusions that you have been treated unfairly or taking a new colleague's computer may prove embarrassing if it was a simple mistake.

**26. B**

This is the right thing to do as it will give you the chance to discuss the matter with your colleague first and clear ambiguity. It is also your responsibility to report the matter to your manager.

**27. C**

This is the right thing to do. Explaining the mistake to the client will help protect the integrity of the message then send the email to the right person.

This is assuming the contents of the email is not catastrophic!  Otherwise choice D may be appropriate.

**28. B**

As a professional you need to find out more about why your colleague insists on having the postmortem before anything else. This will help when talking to the family as you will be able to provide professional counsel. Your partner may have genuine concerns that need to be addressed.

**29. A**

Choice B should be avoided because by asking the customer to calm down instead of helping them to do so you are indirectly telling them they lack self-control. You will sound impatient and rude.  Choice C, referring to the supervisor may give the customer the impression of giving them the run-around.

**30. C**

Choice C is appropriate as shows that you have empathy. Even if you are not able to help the colleague will feel more relieved as a problem shared is a problem half solved.

## 31. B

This problem should be handled immediately and talking to your colleague addresses the urgency. This will also give the colleague a chance to change if what she did was genuinely by mistake.

## 32. D

Discussing the patient's home circumstances with his general practitioner before making any promises to him is the right thing to do. This will help you avoid giving false promises to the patient if his home circumstances are not conducive for his condition. The general practitioner will also advise on the right time to take him home.

## 33. B

This is the most effective response.  You are satisfying the customer's needs the best way you can.

This is a possible solution and a reasonable response; however, you are not giving a direct help and an easy solution. In addition, you want to keep the customer.

## 34. B

Communication is especially important in business environments. Being attentive while communicating you can avoid confusion and misinterpretation. Clear communication leads to better performance.

Although it sounds quite okay to practice yoga, choice A, not all employees understand what it is and the benefits, and may not be interested.

## 35. A

Everybody wants to feel important. By ensuring that the employees feel involved, you keep morale and productivity up.

Leadership styles vary greatly but the sure thing is being bossy to employees leads to reduced productivity. Asserting control or dictating makes people defensive and resist.

## 36. C

This is a challenging situation and getting everyone on board to solve is very important.

Choices A, B and D, are moving ahead blindly.

**37. A**
People buy things because they want the benefits.  This is the only way to convince someone to buy.

The other choices, increasing pressure (hard-sell as choice B) ignoring objections, (choice C) don't work in the long term.

**38. C**
You are being blamed, and fair or not this is the reality.  The first step is to strategize.  Maybe this can be solved with a new strategy and maybe not.

Blaming the supervisor back doesn't solve the problem (choice A).  Going over the supervisor's head, choice B, maybe a good strategy for your next step, but not initially.

**39. A**
It's important to make your side of the story known as a way to avoid confusion and misinterpretation.

By blaming and accusing others you don't help yourself.

**40. A**
The first step in dealing with difficult people is to stay calm and understand their point of view.  After that you can start to build rapport.

Choice C, reporting to your supervisor you can't work with them may be a second step but basically doesn't solve the problem.  Choice D, ignoring their unhelpful behavior, depends on how serious it is – if it is minor this may be OK.  However, Choice A, is the best choice because you are going to have to get along with them.

# WCPT

## SENTENCE ORDER

### 1. E A B D C

Chronologically, sentence E is first, due to the reference to Manning's college career. Sentence A has to follow because it discusses what he did after graduation. Sentence B follows because it directly refers to his NFL career and indicates that more is to come. Sentence D talks about his time with the Colts and the year 2007. Sentence C chronologically must be last because it mentions the year 2010.

### 2. B E C A D

Sentence B includes the clue "first" which denotes its place chronologically. Sentence E contains more detail about the first coaster. Sentence C uses a transition to hint that it comes after the first coaster. Sentence A includes the year 2000 which chronologically comes after 2003. Sentence D concludes the paragraph.

### 3. B E A D C

Sentence B should be first because it continues the ideas from the topic sentence. Sentence E is next because of the transition, "first." Sentence A contains the transition, "another." Sentence D contains the final way to improve on the field. Sentence C contains the conclusion and wraps up the three major ideas.

### 4. D A B C E

Sentence D is first because it describes what an ultra-marathon is. Sentence A is second because it provides more detail about ultra-marathons. Sentence B begins with the word "one" which denotes it is the first special detail. Sentence C takes ultra-marathons a bit farther and adds onto the distances mentioned in Sentence B. Sentence E is last because it gives the final step in ultra-marathon running.

## 5. B E D A C

Sentence B contains general information about wind farms, which are mentioned in the topic sentence. Sentence E provides more specific details about the wind farm turbines. Sentence D goes into greater detail about the height of the turbines. Sentence A refers back to the height of the turbines mentioned in D. Sentence C completes the sentence by explaining why the height is so important.

# READING AND SENTENCE CORRECTION

## 1. D
This question tests the reader's summarization skills. The other choices A, B, and C focus on portions of the second paragraph that are too narrow and do not relate to the specific portion of text in question. The complexity of the sentence may mislead students into selecting one of these answers, but rearranging or restating the sentence will lead the reader to the correct answer. In addition, choice A makes an assumption that may or may not be true about the intentions of the company, choice B focuses on one product rather than the idea of the products, and choice C makes an assumption about women that may or may not be true and is not supported by the text.

## 2. A
This question tests reader's vocabulary and summarization skills. This phrase, used by the author, may seem flippant and dismissive if readers focus on the word "whatever" and misinterpret it as a popular, colloquial term. In this way, Choices B and C may mislead the reader to selecting one of them by including the terms "unimportant" and "stupid," respectively. Choice D is a similar misreading, but doesn't make sense when the phrase is at the beginning of the passage and the entire passage is on media messages. Choice A is literarily and contextually appropriate, and the reader can understand that the author would like to keep the introduction focused on the topic the passage is going to discuss.

## 3. C

This question tests the reader's summarization skills. The entire passage is leading up to the idea that the president of the US may not have had grounds to assert his Fourteen Points when other countries had lost so much. Choice A is pretty directly inferred by the text, but it does not adequately summarize what the entire passage is trying to communicate. Choice B may also be inferred by the passage when it says that the war is "imminent," but it does not represent the entire message, either. The passage does seem to be in praise of FDR, or at least in respect of him, but it does not in any way claim that he is the smartest president, nor does this represent the many other points included. Choice C is then the obvious answer, and most directly relates to the closing sentences which it rewords.

# CORRECTING SENTENCES

## 4. B

Sentence 4 is a fragment.  "Not to mention resolving the conflicts between warring nations."

This sentence is essentially a verbal phrase of the word "resolve" which does not have a main clause as part of the sentence. It is the extension of the sentence preceding it which contains the main clause and does make sense as it stands after the sentence with the main clause. However, since it does not have the main clause in its own structure, it is a sentence fragment.

## 5. A

The following changes to sentence 6 would focus attention on the main idea in paragraph 2.  "Yet, the technology behind the atom bomb essentially had the power of resolving the war itself which scientists like him failed to convey."

The use of the connector "No matter what" in the original sentence is irrelevant given the sense expressed in both the sentences it connects. Taking the context of paragraph into consideration, the use of the connector "Yet" complements the sense expressed in both the sentences.

**6. B**

Suggested changes for sentence 5, "For instance, the atom bomb was developed during the Second World War by the recommendations of the great Albert Einstein - who is accepted as the father of modern physics - in fear of the Germans developing it and using on the Allies."

The original sentence lacks a comma after the thought extension phrase "For instance." Also, the use of dash to link two or more ideas and make a point has been incomplete.

**7. C**

The following sentence, if inserted before sentence 7, would best illustrate the main idea of the passage, "Nuclear fission that is used in the fuelling of the bomb, has the capacity to produce electrical energy which has turned out to be a major alternative later in the Twentieth Century."

The main idea of the passage is the misuse of science regarding the development of the atom bomb during the Second World War, whereas it could effectively be used in meeting the energy demands of the countries involved in the war. This is expressed explicitly in the sentence offered in choice C, which is at the same time coherent with the seventh and eighth sentence between which it is being suggested to be placed. Other choices either lack coherence or are less relevant.

**8. A**

Sentence 4 is a fragment.  "Which I doubt belongs to any <u>other</u> person. "

This sentence is an extension of the sentence preceding it. It does not complete the thought when alone, and is thus a sentence fragment.

**9. A**

Sentence 3 sentence is not consistent with the author's purpose.  "For example, for an air stewardess position, girls have to be no more than 163 cm tall; whereas for jobs in foreign affairs, Chinese diplomats are required to match their foreign counterparts."

The passage talks about the people who want to increase their height by undergoing a surgery and points out the minimum height requirements for getting a job that they wish to work in. However, the expression "no more than 163 cm tall" is a statment about a maximum not a minimum.   In addition, the sentence refers to Chinese diplomats who must 'match' the height of their foreign counterparts, which could be taller, and hence require surgery, or could be shorter and not require surgery.

## 10. B
The following sentence, if inserted after sentence 7, would best illustrate the main idea of the passage, "This artificial way of gaining height is turning out to be a new trend among the new generation in height conscious China."

The paragraph discusses about the application of leg surgery among Chinese young people to increase their height. This is best reflected in the sentence suggested in choice B which also contributes to the cohesion of the second paragraph as well as allowing a smooth transition between the second and third paragraph.

## 11. B
Suggested changes to sentence 8,  "Even parents approve of the idea, being fully aware of all the complications and they are willing to finance such a sophisticated surgery."

The usage of vocabulary is incorrect in this sentence. The word "complexity" is an adjective noun used to describe detailed aspects of a given subject which is less relevant here. The word "labyrinth" is also incorrect in this context. The correct counterpart for "complexity" here, would be "complications" which takes into account the length of the surgery itself and the agony, sacrifice and the commitment associated with it, all in one. Also the word "sophisticated", as suggested in choices B and C in the place of "labyrinth" is more appropriate as it hints about the details of the surgery. Choice B offers both changes.

## 12. A
Sentence 4 is a fragment.  "Which I doubt belongs to any other person. "

This sentence is an extension of the sentence preceding it. It does not complete the thought when alone and is thus a sentence fragment.

## 13. D

Sentence 9 is the least relevant to the main idea of the second paragraph. "He is panicked by street dogs and neighbors' cats and to avoid them, he crosses to the other side of the street every now and then."

The second paragraph mainly talks about Luke's odd behavior while in a moving in a crowd, but sentence 9 shifts the subject to his strategy when he encounters cats and dog in the streets.

## 14. C

Sentence 4 contains a redundant phrase. "Which I doubt any other person belongs to other than him."

In this sentence the second "other" is redundant. It can be omitted.

## 15. B

The following sentence, if inserted before sentence 1, would best illustrate the main idea of the passage. "But that does not bother him; rather he always seems to be happy in being able to utter those two words."

The passage starts with the speculation that Luke is probably the only person happy with his peculiar character and style of living. This is reflected in the sentence which is suggested to be added as the last sentence. Other choices do not offer the same relevance and coherence.

## 16. D

Sentence 6 is a fragment, "But for a day only."

This sentence fails to complete a thought when it stands alone. It is complementary as a thought extension to the previous sentence though and makes perfect sense when it is preceded by that. Since it neither has a noun clause, nor a verbal, it is a sentence fragment.

**17. C**

Sentence 8 is not consistent with author's purpose. "But as they came to know him closely, they were disappointed he would only occupy Mr. Drodsky's position for  two weeks."

In sentence 6, the author indicates that the new teacher is replacing Mr. Drodsky for one day only. However, in sentence 8, it is clearly stated that he will be replacing him for two weeks, contradicting his earlier statement.

**18. A**

Suggested changes to sentence 16, "Coming from a public school in New Jersey, Ray had never seen students 'tamed' to such narrow, disparate discipline in his six years of experience as a music teacher."

The original sentence contains the wrong usage of the word "desperate." The use of the homophone "disparate" is more suited to express the distinct trait of the students in the new school he has joined. The right modification is suggested in choice A and all other choices offer incorrect changes.

**19. D**

Sentence 7 contains non-standard usage, "Aa you wiss me, chilsren?"

This sentence refers to Mr. Drodsky's Eastern European accent that can be considered as non-standard usage. Although strictly incorrect, it is permissible stylistically to illustrate his accent.

**20. D**

Sentence 5 is a fragment.  "Hanging in between two sides of the wall near one corner of the store room which they rarely open, a magnificent piece of art left half woven and still being worked on."

This sentence does not express a complete thought since it does not have a verbal clause. A possible revision would be: "Hanging between two walls near one corner of the store room , lies a magnificent piece of art left half woven and still being worked on."

# VOCABULARY

**1. B**
**Heinous:** adj. shocking, terrible or wicked.

**2. A**
**Harbinger:** n. a person of thing that tells or announces the coming of someone or something

**3. B**
**Judicious:** Having, or characterized by, good judgment or sound thinking.

**4. B**
**Ethanol:**  n. a colorless volatile flammable liquid C2H6O.

**5. A**
**Respiratory:** adj. Of, relating to, or affecting respiration or the organs of respiration.

**6. B**
**Inherent:** Naturally a part or consequence of something.

**7. A**
**Vapid:** adj. tasteless or bland.

**8. C**
**Waif:** n. homeless child or stray.

**9. D**
**Homologous:** adj. similar or identical.

**10. B**
**Obsolete:** adj. no longer in use; gone into disuse; disused or neglected.

**11. A**
**Rankle:** v. To cause irritation or deep bitterness.

**12. D**
**Reusable**

## 13. C
**Torpid:** adj. Lazy, lethargic or apathetic.

## 14. A
**Gregarious:** adj. Describing one who enjoys being in crowds and socializing.

## 15. B
**Mutation:** n. a change or alteration.

## 16. C
**Lithe:** adj. flexible or pliant.

## 17. A
**Resent:** v. to express displeasure or indignation.

## 18. A
**Immaterial:** irrelevant not having substance or matter.

## 19. A
**Impeccable:** adj. perfect, no faults or errors.

## 20. B
**Pudgy:** adj. fat, plump or overweight.

# ENGLISH

## 1. C
The semicolon is used in a list where the list items have internal punctuation, such as "Key West, Florida."

## 2. C
The semicolon links independent clauses. An independent clause can form a complete sentence by itself.

## 3. A
The semicolon links independent clauses with a conjunction (However).

## 4. B
The sentence is correct. The semicolon links independent

clauses.  An independent clause can form a complete sentence by itself.

## 5. B
Double negative sentence.  In double negative sentences, one negatives is replaced with "any."

## 6. A
The third conditional is used for talking about an unreal situation (that did not happen) in the past.  For example, "If I had studied harder, [if clause] I would have passed the exam [main clause].  Which is the same as, "I failed the exam, because I didn't study hard enough."

## 7. D
Present perfect.  You cannot use the Present Perfect with specific time expressions such as: yesterday, one year ago, last week, when I was a child, at that moment, that day, one day, etc. The Present Perfect is used with unspecific expressions such as: ever, never, once, many times, several times, before, so far, already, yet, etc.

## 8. C
Bring vs. Take.  Usage depends on your location. Something coming your way is brought to you. Something going away is taken from you.
## 9. A
The sentence is correct.  Went vs. Gone.  Went is the simple past tense.  Gone is used in the past perfect.

## 10. B
Fewer vs. Less.  'Fewer' is used with countables and 'less' is used with uncountables.

## 11. D
Its vs. It's.  'It's' is a contraction for it is or it has.  'Its' is a possessive pronoun meaning, more or less, of 'it,' or belonging to 'it.'

## 12. D
When using 'however,' place a comma before and after.

## 13. B

"Who" is the best choice because the sentence refers to a person.

## 14. A

Past perfect is the correct form because it refers to something that happened in the past (he was the greatest inventor) and is still true today.

## 15. C

The superlative "hottest" is used when expressing the highest degree, or a degree greater than that of anything it is compared with.

## 16. D

When comparing two, use 'the taller.' When comparing more than two, use 'the tallest.'

## 17. B

Here the word "sale" is used as a "word" and not as a word in the sentence, so quotation marks are used.

## 18. C

His father is a poet and a novelist. It is necessary to use 'a' twice in this sentence for the two distinct things.

## 19. C

Titles of short stories are enclosed in quotation marks, and commas always go inside quotation marks.

## 20. B

Present tense, "ran well" is correct. "Ran good" is never correct.

## 21. D

Punctuation always goes inside quotation marks.

## 22. D

Healthful vs. Healthy. 'Healthy' is used to describe something that is of good for your health and 'healthful' refers to habits or types.

### 23. A

In vs. Into. 'In' a room means inside.  'Into' refers to movement or action.

### 24. C

Lay vs. Lie.  Lie requires an object and lay does not.  So you can lie down, (no object. and you lay a book on the floor.

### 25. A

The third conditional is used for talking about an unreal situation (that did not happen) in the past.  For example, "If I had studied harder, [if clause] I would have passed the exam [main clause].  Which is the same as, "I failed the exam, because I didn't study hard enough."

### 26. A

Learn vs. Teach.  Learning is what students do, and teaching is what teachers do.

### 27. B

Lose vs. Loose. Lose is to no longer have, or to lose a race. Loose is not tied or able to move freely.

### 28. D

Persecute vs. Prosecute.  To prosecute is to have a legal claim against someone and to persecute is to harass.

### 29. A

Precede vs. Proceed.  To precede is to go first or in front of. To proceed is to go forward.

### 30. A

Quoted speech is not capitalized.

### 31. A

The sentence is correct.  Periods and events are capitalized but not century numbers.

### 32. C

Brand names are capitalized.

### 33. B

Generic terms such as 'french fries' are not capitalized. Brand names are capitalized.

**34. C**

The names of sports teams, as proper nouns, are capitalized. In this sentence, the full name is capitalized, Blue Jays.

**35. A**

The sentence is correct.  North, South, East, and West when used as sections of the country, but not as compass directions.

# CONCLUSION

CONGRATULATIONS! You have made it this far because you have applied yourself diligently to practicing for the exam and no doubt improved your potential score considerably! Getting into a good school is a huge step in a journey that might be challenging at times but will be many times more rewarding and fulfilling. That is why being prepared is so important.

Study then Practice and then Succeed!

**Good Luck!**

## REGISTER FOR FREE UPDATES AND MORE PRACTICE TEST QUESTIONS

Register your purchase at
https://www.test-preparation.ca/register/
for updates, free test tips and more practice test questions.

# Visit us Online